Tickle H

Your Hands-On Gu

Dr. Sadie Allison

Illustrated by Steve Lee

ticklekitty®
Go love yourself.™

ticklekitty.com
San Francisco

Author: Dr. Sadie Allison
Editor-In-Chief: Rich Lippman
Creative Director: Richard G. Martinez
Editor: Joe Azar
Book Design: ArtThug (ArtThug.com)

Illustrator: Steve Lee
Logo Design: Todd LaRose
Cover/Author Photos: Richard G. Martinez

Published by Tickle Kitty, Inc.
3701 Sacramento Street #107
San Francisco, CA 94118
United States
Fax: 1-(415) 876-1900
http://www.ticklekitty.com

Please Note
This book is intended for educational and entertainment purposes only. Neither the Author, Illustrator, nor Publisher is responsible for the use or misuse of any sexual techniques or devices discussed here, or for any loss, damage, injury or ailment caused by reliance on any information contained in this book. Please use common sense. If you have any health issues or other concerns, you should consult a qualified healthcare professional or licensed therapist BEFORE trying any techniques or devices. Please read the Appendix for tips on safer sex, and consult a physician or a qualified healthcare professional if you have any further questions. Be sure to read and carefully follow all instructions that come with any sexual aids you decide to use. The mention of any product or service in this book does not constitute an endorsement. Trademarks and service marks used are the property of their respective owners.

Table Of Contents

Fore Play

Welcome to the book that's all about your guy's pickle.

Whether it's sweet, dill, candied or kosher—now that you're between the covers, let's call it precisely what it is: *a penis.*

For all of society's fixations and infatuations, it's odd there's never been an instructional handbook on the penis for the millions who'd surely appreciate it: women. Haven't *you* got a few dangling penis questions you've always been curious to get to the bottom of?

Such as, *"What does he REALLY want me to do to it?"*

Then fasten your seatbelt! I'm about to bring you as close to understanding the penis as you can get without actually having one. As America's Pleasure Coach, I've spent years looking behind the bulge—asking, touching, playing, investigating, fondling— and I'm here to report to you on *everything* I've uncovered.

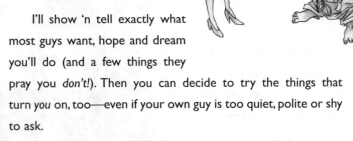

I'll show 'n tell exactly what most guys want, hope and dream you'll do (and a few things they pray you *don't!*). Then you can decide to try the things that turn *you* on, too—even if your own guy is too quiet, polite or shy to ask.

You have my personal guarantee: He won't know what hit him—and what got into you! ♥

X's and O's,

Dr. Sadie Allison

Dr. Sadie

Welcome To Penis School!

Class is now in session. I'm Sadie, your Personal Pleasure Coach, and I'll be showing you some pretty exciting stuff.

So please get comfortable, open your mind, let go of those inhibitions, and get ready to experience orgasmic new passions.

If penis pleasing is relatively new to you, *Congratulations!* You're about to discover the secrets some women never learn in a lifetime. If you're experienced, *Welcome!* You're sure to see lots of exotic new

W

techniques that will melt your lover into your hands. If you're gay—*Hel-LOo-o!* You'll pick up some great pointers here, too. And if you're the object of our affection—*come up here so the whole class can admire you!*

Penis School has no tests and no report cards (but pop quizzes may spring up at any time!). Try only what you're comfortable doing, and advance at your own pace. Talk. Experiment. Laugh. Love. Practice. Improvise. Orgasm. And when you find what works for him—and you—*do it again!*

Whether you're dating for now or mating for life, no matter what your looks, age or physique, you're going to learn how to keep "that glow" in your lover's eyes while you start feeling even sexier inside. And whether your relationship is bumpy or blissful, you'll see how it can be a lot more loving and affectionate— inside the bedroom and out.

So relax. Take a deep breath and begin on the next page. I hope you'll enjoy attending Penis School as much as you enjoy doing the homework! ♥

> **IMPORTANT:** The first lesson of Penis School is **safer sex.** Be sure to read, understand and practice everything in the Appendix before engaging in any sexplay.

Let's Talk About You

I'll bet you could fill a week's worth of Happy Hours telling me about all the headaches that bring you down.

But are you letting those daily distractions follow you into the bedroom? Do you and your guy climb into bed every night only to conk out? What happened to love? What happened to lovemaking? What's happening to your love life?

What if—out of the blue—you initiate a master plan to rekindle your love life? What if the centerpiece is a daring new passion for your guy's penis? What if you start dazzling him with exotic new strokes, touches and licks that render him speechless with mind-blowing orgasms? Would you get his attention? Would you reignite desire? Do I even have to ask?!?

Yet I guarantee that NONE of my erotic advice will work for you if you can't put yourself into "The Moment." So ask yourself: are passion, pleasure, romance, affection, love and orgasms what you want in your life?

Good! Then let's get into "The Moment."

Sharpen Your Pleasure Focus

Ohhh, that feels good … I wonder why the car was making that funny noise … Yes!! More of that… What time are the kids coming home?… Faster, faster, harder, THERE!… I hope he isn't staring at my butt...

Does your mind scan faster than a couch potato with a TV remote? Would you agree it's difficult to enjoy sex when worries, anxieties and hang-ups keep crashing your party? You've come down with a case of the PITs—Pleasure Interrupting Thoughts —a common problem among both women and men.

What's the answer? Start making a conscious effort to tune out the negative PITs at the *exact* moment they intrude. Don't let them rob you of your lusty moments together. Focus only on how good you're feeling—and how good you make him feel. That's what being in "The Moment" means—it's truly empowering.

Get Out Of The PITs

Are you battling any of the following Pleasure Interrupting Thoughts? Then here are some easy ways to turn them around. Remember: focusing on your PITs only draws attention to them. Instead, draw attention only to what turns you on!

"I can't relax." Create your own personal oasis: Lock the door. Unplug the phone. Mute the message machine. Turn off the TV, cell and computer. Treat yourself to a hot bubble bath. Light a scented candle, pop in your favorite CD and feel the groove. Read an erotic story. Pleasure yourself.

"Nice girls don't." *Au contraire:* nice girls DO—you may simply be ready to move on to the next phase of your adult life. Sexual wants and needs can change over the years, so relax and discover the joy that pleasing your partner will bring you in return. *Remember:* there's nothing "dirty" about sex—it's one of life's greatest gifts to you.

"I'm too fat." Your guy isn't going to care about your thighs while your luscious lips are working your magic on him. Being sexy isn't about how you look. It's about attitude, self-confidence and feeling sexy inside.

"I'm afraid I may not like it." Fear usually comes from the unknown, so you may need to turn and simply face your fears. Go slowly and talk about your feelings if you need to. You may be surprised to discover you really enjoy it.

"I don't like the sight of his penis." Then don't look! Turn out the lights and let your skills take over. Add in soft light as you get more comfortable. Try to gain a new appreciation for his penis. After all, it's permanently attached.

"He doesn't smell great." Then bathe before sex—together! Wash his penis for him and make sure you rinse him completely of soap (it tastes gross). Suggest a sensual shave to start him smelling even sweeter! (See Chapter 5.)

"I don't like his taste or texture." Then mask it with fruit-flavored lubes or something good from the kitchen—like maple syrup!

"I don't know how to start." You've already taken a giant step forward by opening this book. Just pick an easy starter technique that looks inviting—and try it. Guys may not always tell you, but most of them LOVE when their woman initiates sexplay.

Reveal Your Sexual Power

Are you confident in your lovemaking? Comfortable expressing yourself erotically? Sexually equal with your partner?

This guidebook is about empowering you to enjoy sex because you want to please *yourself*—not simply please your guy. You'll quickly discover that losing your inhibitions can be a liberating experience. Finding more passion in your life can bring more passion back to you. Giving new pleasure to the one you adore can multiply many times over.

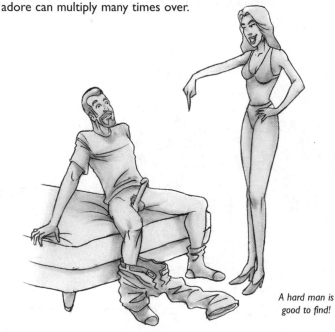

A hard man is good to find!

Whether you realize it or not, inner beauty radiates outward. When you feel good about yourself, your lover will feel good about you, too. Take this opportunity to make a fresh start to reveal your full sexual power—and revel in it!

Good Sex Starts At The Lips

I mean communicating! Real, honest, open, two-way talk about what's on your minds. But since many guys need help in the communication department—it may be up to you to break the ice.

Let's Talk About *You*

Venturing into these frozen waters can be difficult—even a bit embarrassing. But once you start talking, you can each begin to open up about any issues that may run under the surface. Remember: talking about sex doesn't ruin a romance—it rescues it.

What can you discover? Only what's on each other's mind! Perhaps he's harboring issues about size, scent, taste, erection quality or ejaculation control. Or could you be coping with dryness, discomfort or no orgasms? The news may not all be negative—perhaps you're both ready for more oral sex, new positions, greater variety or even a vibrating sex toy!

Airing your issues in a positive light, rather than letting them linger unexamined, can lead to a much healthier relationship. You'll be able to stop all that guessing about what may be wrong. Then you can agree on solutions that bring you closer together. And if any issues run deeper than you thought, you can sort things out by talking to a qualified therapist.

Touch Each Other With Words

Good communication isn't just for exploring issues. It's for exploding passion! Just choose the right words, and you'll make your partner feel wanted, desired and loved as you stimulate a deeply intense connection.

But where do you start? Try whispering one or two of these icebreakers that'll send a thrill up and down his spine. Reassure him that everything each of you says will stay just between the two of you:

♥ "What would *you* like to try tonight?"

♥ "It turns me on to talk about fantasies. Tell me one of yours…"

♥ "Can I tell you what turns *me* on?"

♥ "Do you like when I do this…or *this*?"

Once you break the code of silence, the words start flowing, and the passion starts showing. And if yesterday's desire for slow 'n sensual has now become today's craving for fast 'n furious, words can be the best passion catalyst.

Ever talk about sexy things *outside* the bedroom? Try it over a romantic dinner, at the park or even on a long walk. Choose non-intimidating places where you can't easily be overheard— unless that's what you want!

Sadie Sez:

A surefire conversation starter. Frustrated by a stubborn non-talker? Try this: bookmark your favorite sections in this book, and set it out for him where you know he'll find it—in the bathroom!

Untying your tongues will allow you to do many more sexy things with them—and we'll get to that in Chapter 4.

A Word About Dirty Words

The English language has more vivid words for sex than just about any other topic. But as you've probably noticed, most of the politically correct words for sex also drain the joy right out of it.

"OH GOD EJACULATE INSIDE ME!" sounds a bit too dorky. And "CUM" is a bit too porny. So I've tried to select words for this book that you might say in quiet conversation with your closest friends, and in the heat of passion with your lover.

You'll also notice that my nouns and verbs get hotter as the action gets hotter. Just like yours can, too!

What's In It For You?

A handjob and a blowjob shouldn't be a job. They should be a pleasure, as well as erotic, sensual, fun and fulfilling. They're the ultimate bond, and if they aren't currently part of your repertoire, or have somehow dropped out of your routine, I'm here to help you find fresh inspiration.

So lend me your ears—as well as your hands and mouth!

Why not check with your best friends and see what they know about the subject. Set up a *Sex and the City* lunch date! You know: finger food, cosmopolitans and people-watching—with three of your closest girlfriends. And bring this book! By the second cosmo, you'll learn exactly what your friends and their guys love doing behind closed doors (and in wide-open spaces!).

It's a good way to remind yourself what a wonderful pleasure we've all been given to enjoy. Not wicked. Not a sin. But oh so wickedly sinful! ♥

2 Meet The Penis
& The Land
Down Under

Come say hello to someone eager to meet you. He was attracted to you from the very first instant he saw you. And now he's bursting to get to know you better—inside and out!

Meet the penis, your living sex toy.

11

Some women see the penis as a work of art. Others just see it as work. How about you? Everyone can acquire tastes for things they may not appreciate fully at first, like fine wine, spinach, sushi—and penis!

With a fresh look at the penis, you can start enjoying new pleasures beyond your wildest imagination—both giving *and* receiving. You may even have a totally transforming life experience, especially when the lubricant is love.

So come with me on a fun, enjoyable tip-to-testicles tour. I'll show you all the places of interest, pleasure zones, trigger points—and how YOU can get a standing ovation for your reignited energy, creativity and enthusiasm.

The Penis: Your Guided Tour

Penises are fascinating—and fun to play with! And just like vaginas, penises have infinite variations in size, color and shape.

Some are big, some are small, and some will surprise you by how big they become. Some are one shade. Others are two.

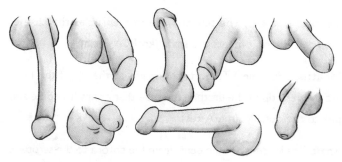

Some get stiff and point to the sky. Others aim at your toes. Some have big heads. Others are knee-slappers. A few swivel around like human joysticks. Others veer to one side. A handful curve up like bananas. Others are straight as arrows. Many are circumcised. And all the rest are not.

The average penis in the USA today measures between 2 to 4 inches soft, and 5 to 7 inches erect, with an erect shaft girth (circumference) of about 4 to 5 inches—all engineered by nature for your pleasure, comfort and satisfaction.

The Official Dick-tionary

Glans ("Head") The top part of the penis that's designed for penetration—and pleasure. (glanz)

Frenulum ("V-Spot") The ultra-sensitive skin that forms a "V" on the underside of the penis, between the head and shaft. (FREN•you•lum)

Corona ("Ridge") The tender ridge that encircles the base of the head where it meets the shaft. (ko•ROW•nah)

Meatus ("Peehole") These two tiny lips at the tip of the head are the very tip of the urethra, the tube that brings his come and pee to the outside. (me•A•tus)

Shaft The longneck of the penis, from the corona to the scrotum.

Prepuce ("Foreskin") The loose hood of skin that covers the head of the penis on an uncircumcised man. (PRE•puce)

Tender Spot The sensitive area where the bottom of the shaft connects to the scrotum.

Scrotum ("Sack") The soft wrinkly pouch that holds the testicles. (SKRO•tum)

Testicles ("Balls") The two round glands that produce the sperm. (TES•tickles)

Ball Seam The vertical line along the middle of the scrotum.

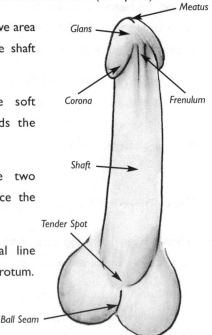

Meatus
Glans
Corona
Frenulum
Shaft
Tender Spot
Ball Seam

Prostate ("Male G-Spot" or "P-Spot") The muscular gland that creates slippery fluid for the semen—also a potent pleasure zone. (PROS•tate)

Pubococcygeus Muscle ("PC Muscle") The muscle that encircles the base of the penis and the anus, that pulses involuntarily at orgasm. (PYOO•bo•cock•SID•jee•us)

Perineum ("Taint") The nerve-ending-rich area of skin between the anus and testicles. (per•IN•eum)

Anus ("Butthole") The nerve-ending-rich opening at the very end of the rectum. (AY•nus)

Rectum The pleasure zone just beyond the anus that responds to pressure. (REK•tum)

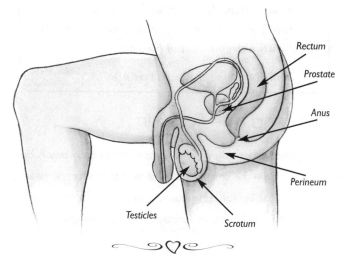

Rectum

Prostate

Anus

Perineum

Testicles

Scrotum

What Is "Penis"?

If you look up "penis" in the average dictionary, here's what you'll find:

The external male organ of copulation that in mammals (including humans) is usually used to expel urine from the body.

Yuck! Who's going to put THAT near their mouth! But why is this fun, sensual, erotic plaything so often described with tongue-twisting clinical terms and pictured with scary medical illustrations?

Perhaps you'll find this definition from Sadie's Dictionary a tad more inviting:

The male love muscle designed to give you the most intensely satisfying gift in the world— orgasms. Your sensual playground to please your lover with extreme sexual pleasure.

Ahhh. *Now bring that penis over here, baby!*

Our Friend, The Foreskin

Whether or not they get to keep it, every baby boy is born with a foreskin—the small hood of skin that covers the head of the penis. Usually for religious or cultural reasons, parents choose to have their baby's foreskin surgically removed shortly after birth. This is called circumcision, and it doesn't reduce penis size, thankfully. In the USA, about 60 percent of newborn males are now circumcised—compared to approximately 15 percent worldwide.

The foreskin actually serves several purposes: it acts like a rolling bearing during intercourse, keeps the head of the penis soft, moist and protected, retains the pheromone sex scent and can give pleasure to both partners during sex. Since foreskins come in varying lengths, some will be visible but most will stretch and "*disappear*" during erections.

If your lover's penis has foreskin, remember these simple precautions:

Be tender. Foreskins will glide up and down along the shaft with each stroking motion, but always be careful—it's thin and delicate and can tear easily. Never grip it too hard, or stretch it too fast or too far.

Foreskin

Go easy. Start pleasing him slowly to avoid sensory overload, since the foreskin is loaded with thousands of nerve endings—and the head of his penis is soft virgin-skin, since it rarely chafes against clothing and zippers.

Wash thoroughly. Cleanliness is ultra important: your partner should glide the skin back and wash underneath with soap and water every day, being sure to rinse out all the soap.

Wipe up! Remind him that if he wipes the head of his penis each time he pees, he'll stay cleaner and fresher for you.

Penis Facts You May Not Know

Most guys naturally "hang" right or left. *They say it feels more comfortable that way. It's okay to ask your guy, "How's it hangin'?"*

Guys can keep an erection for 40 minutes. *Even longer when they're teens—although it's not an Olympic event. Yet.*

Most guys name their penises. *President Johnson. Pope John Pole III, Donald Pump. Ask your guy for his...or name his penis together.*

Many guys think they're smaller than they are. *When they look down, the pubic hair hides some of it—and the perspective from above gives a smaller impression.*

"Shrinkage" is a real phenomenon. *Swimming in cold water shrinks the penis in a New York second!*

> **You can't tell penis size by looking at a guy's hand size.** Or foot size. Or nose size. Or car size. It's hereditary.
>
> **The human penis is among the largest of all the world's primates.** But only when compared to body size (sorry, everyone!)
>
> **Soft size is no indication of hard size.** The smallest penis can grow huge, while the hugest penis can just get stiff.
>
> **Ejaculations can exit the penis at up to 28 mph!** Some guys can actually hit the ceiling, too.

The Land Down Under

There's an entire theme park of pleasure right under his penis. And you've got the ticket to admission.

The "Balls"

Hanging directly below the base of the penis is the *scrotum*, and inside are a pair of *testicles*. Scrotums come in a wide variety of shapes, sizes and textures, and testicles feel like small, round rubber-band balls. All together, this package has generally come to be known as the "balls."

Testicles stay busy night and day producing sperm—200 to 600 million microscopic gene-carrying swimmers for *each*

ejaculation. Testicles are also responsible for pumping out testosterone—the powerful hormone that gives guys beards, deep voices, muscles, sex drive and erection-ability.

Do you know why balls hang outside the body? To keep them cooler and at the perfect temperature for creating sperm. That's why balls tuck themselves snug into the body when it's cold outside. And have you ever noticed that one ball always hangs lower than the other? This keeps them from bumping together when he walks or crosses his legs. Mother Nature thinks of everything!

Expert Ball Handling

With every guy, there's a fine line between erotic and psychotic when you're playing with his balls. Cross that line, and you'll know about it. *Pronto.*

Your best bet is to treat his balls like they're a pair of eggs. Very very delicate eggs. Then you can start getting more playful. Caress them slowly and gently. Listen to his moaning. Read his body language. Be careful not to squeeze too hard or tug his

pubic hair. I'll show you plenty of fun ballplay ideas later in this book that'll make you the best lover ever!

 Sadie Sez:

How sensitive are his balls? Here's an easy way to tell how he likes his balls fondled: ask him to squeeze your breasts with the same pressure he'd like you to apply to his balls. Now you know!

Touch The Taint

Ask a guy to show you his *perineum*, and he'll look at you funny. Ask him to show you his *taint*, and he'll still look at you funny, but he'll probably know what you mean.

Taint is slang for perineum, the flat stretch of skin between the testicles and the anus. Rich in nerve endings, it's where you can feel the root, or bulb, of the penis, which hardens when he gets an erection.

Where did the name taint come from? If you blurt out, "*it ain't* the balls and *it ain't* the butthole," it sounds like you're saying "taint." You can also remember that T.A.I.N.T. stands for The Anus Is Next to This.

Do you ever play with his taint? Try it! It's sensitive but not too delicate, so you can experiment with firmer pressures and different strokes. Want to know how good it feels? Well you have one too, so try playing with your own! It feels good—something most men and women can easily agree on!

Buffing The PC Muscle

You may have read about Kegel exercises designed to strengthen your own PC muscle—which supports your pelvic floor. But did you know guys have the same muscle—and can do strengthening exercises as well?

Why would your guy strengthen it? For better control over his ejaculation timing, stronger orgasms, and new power to send his come flying.

To begin the world's easiest exercise program, he should locate his PC muscle by stopping his pee mid-flow. The muscle tightening he'll feel is the PC muscle in action, and it's even easier if he concentrates on keeping his thigh, back and abdominal muscles relaxed.

To buff up his PC muscle, he can try sets of the following Kegel exercises each day while he's driving or watching TV. ❤

Easy Kegels For Guys

♥ Rhythmically clench and release the pelvic muscle for 10 seconds. Now relax for 5 seconds.

♥ Pulsate quickly for 5 seconds. Relax for 5 seconds.

♥ Clench and hold tight for 30 seconds. Relax for 30 seconds.

Sadie Sez:

ManLand No-Nos. OUCH! Some things don't feel very good down there, and the list changes from guy to guy. What makes one scream with delight might make another scream with pain. But most guys agree on a few things that you can easily avoid.

Penis No-Nos. Icy-cold hands. Coarse palms. Dry mouth. Rough, sharp, dirty fingernails. Excessive yanking, grabbing and biting. Hard scraping with nails, teeth or braces. Catching jewelry in pubic hair. Stroking cross-wise against the tip. Pulling the foreskin back too far. Pulling the penis out past open zipper teeth. And comparing his penis to an ex's.

Testicle No-Nos. Slapping, spanking, squeezing, scratching, fondling or sucking too hard or too rough.

Orgasm No-Nos. Fast stroking right after orgasm, spitting out in disgust, poking the prostate, kissing with a mouthful of come, or suggesting he taste it.

3

He's
Commming!

The male orgasm is a sight to behold. No chance of faking anything here—it's a visual fireworks display, as well as your reward for your generous lovemaking skills and extraordinary touch.

But what goes on behind it all to bring him to this life-affirming moment of physical excitement and bliss? Let's find out.

Easy To Be Hard

Awakening his penis with a gentle touch or your sexy suggestions is truly a marvel of evolution and biology. There's no button you press, no lever you pull—even he has no control over it. Erections are completely autonomic.

But what does it feel like to actually *get* an erection? Some guys describe it as a feeling of rising power and well-being. Others say it feels like pressure building up before the damn bursts—or like a raging bull ready to charge!

Here's what's happening physically: nerves in his spinal cord switch on from sexual thoughts, dreams, hormones, touch. This triggers the opening of arteries that sends blood rushing to his penis, filling up the spongy tissues inside his shaft—the pair of *corpora cavernosa* and *corpus spongiosum*. Simultaneously, muscles at the base of his penis constrict to trap the blood inside, preventing it from leaving through the veins. *Voila!* Instant erection.

All healthy guys get hard when they sleep, when they awaken, and at various unplanned "uh-oh" moments throughout the day. Young guys can pop rock-hard "woodies" in a flash, but as guys age, start-up time gets a bit slower, and erections get a tad softer. Don't worry—it's perfectly normal.

Riding His Sexual Response Cycle

Every mature adult responds to sex in four phases—a cycle originally identified by Masters and Johnson, the groundbreaking sex research team. Although there are many similarities between men and women, understanding the *differences* is what helps you become a better lover.

Phase I: Excitement

You slide your tongue along the edge of his ear. His heart races, his blood pressure rises, his breathing quickens, his nipples harden, his penis grows, pre-ejaculation fluid may appear. This can last from several minutes to several hours, and causes guys to shout across crowded restaurants, "Check, please!!!"

Phase II: Plateau

You kiss deeply as you reach inside his pants. Even higher goes his heart rate, blood pressure, breathing and penis, as his testicles draw up into his body. This can last only a few minutes, although some lovers purposely prolong it for stronger orgasms.

Phase III: Orgasm

Your mouth is working his penis in sync with your soft lubed fingers. While this is the shortest phase (sigh), it's the longest to describe. First, as his seminal fluid begins rapidly pooling at the base of his penis, *nothing on earth* can stop him from coming. His muscles tighten, his anus contracts and his skin flushes, as he pumps out his semen in rhythmic spurts of extreme pleasure.

At first, his semen doesn't overflow like just-popped champagne—it must still travel the entire length of his erect penis. Propelled by his PC muscle, his bursts feel, well, *orgasmic*, with about 4/5ths of a second in between each one. By the fourth burst, the gap between them is increasing, their intensity is tapering off, and the ride is nearing its end.

Even though he'll tell you he mostly feels his orgasms in his genitals, it's a total body event. His brain waves dance, his body's muscles tense, he tingles all over, and his expression can look like he just whacked his thumb with a hammer (but *you* know better!).

Phase IV: Resolution

His mind and body relax. His testicles emerge from his body, his scrotum becomes looser, his penis goes half-erect, then soft—and it's impossible right now to restart the cycle. This can last from a few minutes to a few days, depending on his age and health. What a fine time to discover how skilled he is with his hands, lips and tongue!

Liquid Love

Guys tend to be proud of their come. They love giving it to you, showing it to you, showering you with it, and watching you receive it. Here's how it appears:

Love Drops. Also known as "pre-ejaculation" or "pre-come," this liquid may ooze out of his penis long before he orgasms. It can be clear or white, even a little bubbly—and it's slippery, so it provides extra lubrication. While some guys produce a lot, others can go their entire lives without producing any. Either way, it's totally normal.

 Sadie Sez:

Ejaculation vs. orgasm. Contrary to popular belief, ejaculation and orgasm are not one and the same, although they usually happen together. Ejaculation is the physical act; orgasm is the pleasurable feeling.

Love Juice. Also known as "semen" or "come," this is his ejaculate, and it can be thick, watery, goopy, clear or white. The intensity which it bursts forth is different from guy to guy, from day to day, from mood to mood. His come may simply dribble out, or shoot far across the room in short spurts or medium streams. And if he's *really* turned on, and hasn't orgasmed too recently, be on the lookout for a volcanic eruption!

To Taste Or Not To Taste

It's entirely up to you whether or not you wish to taste his come. If you always avoid it because of a distasteful experience in the past, you may be pleasantly surprised how times and tastes can change!

The unique taste of your guy's come is affected by several factors, but genetics and diet are the most important. It will be warm, and either salty, tangy, sweet, bitter, bleach-y, brie-like—or anything in between.

Want a tastier guy? Here are the secret ingredients:

Come sweeteners: strawberries, papaya, mango, raspberries, blueberries, pineapple, honey.

Come sourers: garlic, spicy foods, asparagus, cauliflower, broccoli, onions, cigarettes, alcohol, coffee. ♥

Sadie Sez:

Try a smoothie sweetener. Although there's no guarantee this smoothie will work for you (but it did for me), there's no harm in trying—it's part of a balanced breakfast!

- ♥ 2 cups fresh squeezed orange juice
- ♥ 6 hulled strawberries
- ♥ 1/4 cup blueberries
- ♥ 1 cup peaches, sliced
- ♥ 1 banana
- ♥ 1 tsp. powdered sugar
- ♥ 4 ice cubes

Blender on high.

Down the hatch.

Enjoy love juice tonight.

Tickle His Pickle

4 Sights!
Sounds!
Seductions!

I'm going to clue you in on sexual techniques so powerful, I can't believe so many smart, savvy women miss them. What's more, any woman who tries them will instantly have her guy eating out of her hand.

Here they are.

Almost every guy's penis reacts like it's hard-wired directly to two of the most potent parts of his anatomy: his eyes and his ears.

Lusty visuals and sexy sounds will instantly amp up your guy's desire for you. *Way up.* If your sexual encounters now tend to be hush-hush affairs cast in a dull light, you'll be amazed at the transformation you're about to discover in *both* of you!

Over the next several pages, you're going to see how to light up his brain circuits with sights and sounds till they're smoldering hot. Half the fun will be watching his new erotic reactions to you—the other half will simply be enjoying your own.

Setting The Sexy Scene

It isn't necessary to go all out with expensive flowers, exotic bedspreads and antique candelabras—unless you want to. What really matters is creating a comfortable setting that helps the two of you feel sexy, confident and good about yourselves.

Setting the sexy scene mostly means making sure your environment is sex-ready. So pack off the kids. Ship off the roommates. Clear off the bed. And set out the apparel, lubricant, toys, condoms and bubblebath for later.

Stuck at work? Tell the boss you need some time off (for bad behavior!). If there's an hour to spare, try to get in an energy-boosting workout—but leave enough time to bathe, shave, file your nails and apply your makeup.

Set Him To 'Simmer'

Do you know why certain recipes instruct you to simmer rather than boil? Slow cooking gets juices flowing.

Since you're already planning to devour him, why not preset his dial to 'simmer'—as you sear some wicked temptations into his brain. It's easy—pick any two:

♥ Surprise him with a deep, smoldering kiss before he leaves for the day. Look flirtatiously into his eyes. Offer no further explanation.

♥ Record a flirty 'hint' on his voicemail, or text-message him with a few suggestions about what's in store for him.

Sadie Sez:

The best laid plans. Before sending him your flirtatious signals, make certain you're not about to go up against work deadlines, an unbreakable commitment or Game Seven of the World Series.

Tickle His Pickle

♥ Place a heart-pumping call to his cellphone at a moment you know he can't *possibly* return your flirtations.

♥ Send him an email entitled "Your Appointment" and attach a naughty digital picture that the two of you took together. But beware of company-monitored emails!

♥ Place a naughty note in his lunch-bag or jacket pocket or sneak a pair of your perfumed panties in his briefcase.

The Final Countdown

A few extra touches now can lead to lots of sexy touching later:

- ♥ **Lighting.** Set out candles for a soft romantic glow that can also help ease any self-consciousness. Place them far enough away where they can't be tipped over in the heat of passion.

- ♥ **Tunes.** Pre-load your perfect mood music in the CD or MP3 player. Then simply press *play* when the moment's right.

- ♥ **Scent.** Try a light lavender spritz, scented candles or incense to create a magical scent in the room.

- ♥ **Food.** If a romantic meal is on the menu, forgo heavy dishes that weigh you down, and gassy foods that bloat you up.

- ♥ **Bath Prep.** If waterplay is in the picture, draw a bubblebath or ready the shower. Set out a fresh loofah, sensually scented gels and the waterproof vibrator.

Aural Aphrodisiacs

What's the dirtiest thing you ever moaned during sex? If "the lampshade needs dusting" ever crossed your lips, here's a better way to open the pipeline directly into his pleasure center: erotic talking.

Sadie Sez:

Things your guy LOVES to hear. These phrases are going to sound awfully silly if you're reading this in a store. But they're going to sound awfully hot when you say any one of these to your guy in the heat of passion.

Does that feel good, baby?

Do you like when I touch myself here?

I'll do anything for you.

I love your dick in my mouth.

Your touch makes me so hot.

Do you want it faster, softer, tighter…?

You make me so wet.

Please come all over me.

You feel so good inside me.

Mmmmm, you taste good.

Remember: if you're feeling it, say it. Keep it short and breathy. How you say it can be just as important as what you say. And be sure to say the sexiest thing of all: his name.

Sights! Sounds! Seductions!

If talking during sex is new to you—or you feel a bit self-conscious—remember that it's perfectly okay because everything you say is just between the two of you. Once you break the sound barrier, you'll discover that dirty talk can be truly liberating. More than just a big turn-on—you also find out what each of you likes.

Ease into it. Lightly brush your lips against his ear, and softly whisper how good you feel when he touches you.

Try sounds instead of words. Moans, *mmmms, ohhhs* and *ahhhs*—even the noises of kissing, breathing, licking and sucking—are sexy to the ear.

Try words together with sounds. Tell him in a breathy voice what you're about to do to him. *"I'm going to take you in my mouth."* If you feel like you're doing all the talking, ask him a non-yes-or-no question about what he wants you to do, like, *"Where do you want me to lick you now?"*

Honesty is your best aphrodisiac. Say you're hot when you're hot; wet when you're wet; coming when you're coming. Score extra erotic points by breathlessly saying his name. *"Do you want to watch me touch myself, Richard?"* You can even pour out one of your sexual fantasies. Remember, he wants to know.

Look Delicious

Guys are visual creatures. They love to watch action sports, action movies, action television and you—in action.

Your guy is already looking lustily at you during sex. But are you self-consciously covering up, or giving him an erotic eyeful. The less shy you are, the more turned on he'll be.

You can hold him spellbound simply by putting yourself in his visual crosshairs. Try any of these suggestions and enjoy your own visual feast watching how turned-on he'll be:

Dress seductively. Whether his fantasy is slinky lingerie, leather Biker Chick or Ze French Maid, wear your costumes proudly. Even better, buy them too tight so your breasts appear like they're about to fall out! Now do a strip tease for him.

Touch yourself. Pinch your nipples, squeeze your breasts, suck your finger, run your hands through your hair. It'll feel good to you—and look great to him.

Strike a pose. You know your greatest assets. Position yourself to show them off! Let him see you're playful and confident—and that you know what he likes.

Live in the moment. Let your body language speak for you—your glistening skin, erotic expressions, luscious lips, arched back, thrusting hips. When he sees *you're* turned on, he'll be even more turned on.

Pleasure yourself. There are few sights sexier to a guy than to watch his woman masturbate for him. The sight of you touching your beautiful vagina will send your guy out of his mind.

Eyes Wide Open

Would you like to knock your guy's socks off so far, they'll wash, dry and fold themselves, too? Then take a deep breath, open up your mind, and consider this:

Adult videos.

Gulp! If you're like many women, you instantly flashed back to cheesy porn scenes from the '70's, featuring gross guys with caveman body hair doing sexual acrobatics to the world's funkiest soundtrack.

Before you say, "two thumbs down," hear me out.

Times have changed. Some of today's productions, while certainly not Hollywood blockbusters, have now become higher

quality entertainment, featuring sexier, more appealing actors who may easily arouse your interest, too.

But why should you watch adult videos? *It's what your guy wants.*

Most every guy I've ever met will jump at the chance to watch an adult video with his lover. Even if he's never said it out loud, your guy is no exception (and if he is, he'll tell you).

Want proof? Next time you're lying in bed, say in a soft, innocent tone, *"I'm a little curious to watch an adult video with you."* If he doesn't immediately kiss you on the lips—or on the feet— it's because he's too busy thanking his lucky stars to be with such a giving and generous lover.

Getting Past "Gross!"

Has your guy ever skipped hanging out with his buddies or missed a big football game just to go with you to an unmanly event? Could it be your turn to try something *he* really wants—especially if it ultimately brings *you* pleasure? Here's how to ease any anxiety.

Start with an open mind. There's nothing to be intimidated by, not a thing to be jealous about, no one you're being compared to. This is just for your own private viewing pleasure on a two-dimensional TV screen that can be switched off at the touch of a button.

Sadie Sez:

Setting video boundaries. Adult videos should be used to lift up your love life, not create a crutch. You should both agree on what types of adult entertainment you'll watch, and how often they should be watched. Remember: there's no obligation to watch any of them, and either of you should have the power to pull the plug.

It's no big deal, really. It's just another couple having sex. If you don't like the particular couple you're watching, fast forward to the next couple. If the words or sounds bother you, click 'mute' and play your favorite music and simply let the video run as background visuals.

They're better then ever. Did you know that many adult videos now come with no talky backstories—just erotic scenes? Just find the genres that turn you on, and give the fast forward button a rest.

You might actually like it. *Whoa!* Could you actually find yourself getting wet watching a real hunk working some extraordinary magic with his tongue? What if...while you're watching...your own guy starts working the same magic on you? Have you ever had an explosive orgasm like *THAT*?

You could learn something. If the action doesn't move you, try watching it strictly as an educational video you can secretly title, *Moves to Mimic*.

You can satisfy his fantasies. Is he into anything you're not particularly fond of? Foot love? Light bondage? Anal sex? Then select a video that plays to his fetishes, and bypass the part about your own participation. He's happy—and you're off the hook. And don't neglect watching movies featuring fetishes of your own! ❤

 Sadie Sez:

Mute your cynical soundtrack. There's no bigger turn-off for a guy than to hear his woman picking apart the adult video he's enjoying. Sure they're acting. Sure those are fake breasts. Sure that was a "real" orgasm. Surely you can find something better to do with your mouth!

5

Hair Today—
Gone
Tomorrow

Pubic hair first appears at adolescence, and never stops growing. Whether you prefer your partner's pubic hair curly, fine and soft—or thick, course and bushy—his fur lining is determined entirely by his genetic makeup. Admire it in the wild. Or groom it to your liking.

Tickle His Pickle

It's believed that pubic hair is designed to catch and hold pheromones, his powerful sex-attractant scent you may subconsciously detect. It also holds his powerful anti-attractant, sweat, which you may also detect, not so subconsciously. By trimming or shaving him, he should start smelling fresher, looking tidier—and giving you less wiry underbrush to blaze trails through.

It's okay to suggest a little trim, or even a full shave-down. He may discover he likes the look, as well as the virgin feeling of your lips, tongue and labia on his formerly bush-covered real estate.

Why not make a special occasion out of this, and do the trimming for him?

Sadie Sez:

The sweet smell of success. Trimmed, shaven, or unshorn, for the sweetest smelling experience, ask him to wash and rinse thoroughly with soap and water every day. After all, won't you want to spend more time in the southland when the air is fresh and clean?

Preparing To Groom

Since you'll be wielding sharp steel cutting tools so close to his precious package, his level of trust in you must be very high. That's why it's especially important there's no clowning around, and you're both completely sober.

Get him in a comfortable, stable position where there's no chance of anyone losing balance. Sit him in the bathroom, stand him in the shower or even lay him down on the couch. Place a towel underneath to act as a drop-cloth, and have a bowl of warm water at-hand for rinsing.

Don't rush! Give yourselves an hour or more to get it right. If he's open to the idea of grooming, but nervous about the blade, you can trim or shave the outer parts and let him handle the delicate areas himself. Have a hand-mirror ready for him, too.

Make sure all your cutting instruments are new or sharp. Choose mild, hypoallergenic shaving gels, lotions and creams—and experiment till you find what works best. Have a jar of aloe vera gel handy to soothe any razor burn, and a tissue to clot any nicks.

Caution: *If he ever has allergic reactions or irritations after shaving his face, then expect them to be even worse down below. Never use hair-dissolving sprays or chemical tear-offs from cheesy late-night infomercials. They're for your own legs.*

The Light Trim

The thickest hair usually covers the pubic bone and encircles the base of the penis. Some hair also grows on the scrotum, on the bottom of the shaft, inside the buttcrack, and up a "happy trail" to his belly button. How much you trim is up to the two of you.

Simply use a pair of scissors—blunt-nosed are safest—or a clean electric beard trimmer (if it's not a plug-in, use fresh batteries for optimum performance). Be careful never to touch the trimmer to the skin of his scrotum.

 Sadie Sez:

Shaving adds length! If he's nervous about grooming, tell him it will make his penis look larger! How? It's an optical illusion because more of his penis is now visible to the naked eye—and I'll bet he won't object if you admire it!

Shape the underbrush to an even, pleasing, stylized length—just comb and tug like a professional stylist to straighten the hair, then trim it off. Stand back and admire your handiwork. Since this should result in less chafing during sex, why not reverse roles and let him give you a light trim, too?

Sometimes even the best trim can look a bit out of place if his entire midsection is hairy. You can blend your trim into the surrounding hair by gliding a double- or triple-edged razor 1/8-inch above his skin. Keep rinsing the blade as soon as it clogs with hair, and use your best artistic sense to feather your work into his outlying areas.

The Clean Shave

For the truly naked look, you can shave everything—base, balls, shaft and butt—right down to his soft smooth skin. Here's how.

Start him off with a light trim (see above), but swoop in closer for a crew-cut. Now ease him into a hot relaxing bath or shower to help set up the hair follicles for smoother shaving. Towel him off from head to toe, stopping for a loving pat-dry in the middle. Now apply plenty of a moisturizing, low-or-no foam shaving product, and wait several minutes for everything to soften.

With a fresh cartridge in the safety razor, you're ready to begin:

♥ **Use a light touch.** No need for a lot of pressure on the razor's handle—it doesn't give a closer shave and it can be extra irritating. If the razor starts to drag, click in a fresh cartridge.

♥ **Shave around the base.** Try to minimize the number of passes with the razor. First shave *with* the grain (the direction the hair grows), then against the grain. Keep rinsing the blade in warm water.

♥ **Shave the balls.** For a smooth, lickable scrotum, the skin should be hanging loose, not withdrawn and frightened. Use your fingertips to gently stretch the skin down, creating a smooth, taut surface that the blade can glide across easily. Apply the light-touch rule above. *Do not rush!*

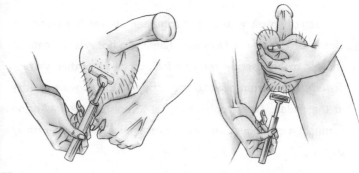

Hair Today—Gone Tomorrow

♥ **Shave the shaft.** Start the blade where the hair begins, and use long, light, strokes to shave in the direction the hair grows.

♥ **Shave between the cheeks.** After a good trimming, carefully glide the razor from the center outward, toward his cheeks. Never shave up, down or inward.

♥ **Ouch!** If you're careful, and your blade stays sharp, he shouldn't get nicked. But if he does, press a tissue firmly against the nick for a couple minutes till it clots. Then apply aloe vera gel.

♥ **The grand finale.** Carefully rinse everything with warm water and pat dry. Apply a non-stinging, alcohol- and fragrance-free, hypoallergenic aftershave balm or gel to soothe and moisturize—but hold off on this till later if you're about to have sex.

♥ **Reduce stubble and itching.** His hair will immediately begin to grow back, along with the irresistible need to scratch himself in public. Shave again to reduce itching, keep reapplying lotion, and assure him the itching will decrease over time. ♥

Tickle His Pickle

6 Slippery Stuff

I'm always curious when a woman tells me she's never used a sex lubricant—or gave up after a ho-hum experience with just one. She doesn't know what she's missing!

53

A good lube is essential for great handjobs and good sex. It'll do more than prevent chafing and irritation—it'll actually "wake up" pleasure receptors in your skin. Touch that feels good before lube feels more alive the instant you apply it. I don't know how any guy could stand a handjob without it!

Good lubes are so widely available, it's easy to find the right one for you and your guy. Look in drugstores and supermarkets near the condoms or feminine-protection sections, and in sex toy stores and lingerie boutiques. Or just go online.

But don't be intimidated by the choices—lightweight, heavy-weight, ultra-thick, water-, silicone-, oil-based, flavored, natural. I'm here to help glide you down the pleasure path to figure out which one you can start slathering all over your guy's penis, your toys, and each other. *C'mon!*

Nature's Lubricant

Did you know you've already got a dispenser full of sex lube with you? Saliva.

This cost-free natural liquid is everyone's instant lube for tongue kissing, but it's often overlooked as a great starter lube for handjobs. Of course, most people simply can't keep up with the demand, so they have a bottle of lube on hand, too.

To keep your saliva flowing, remember to drink plenty of water throughout the day, and keep a glass by the bedside to wet your mouth. To increase your liquid output, try massaging yourself right under the jaw to jumpstart your salivary glands, or suck on sour candy.

Water-Based Lubes

H_2O is necessary for life, and now it's essential for the slipperiest sex, too.

Water-based lubricants are today's best, safest starter lubes. They come in free-flowing liquids, or longer-lasting jellies and gels; and in fruity flavors to add zest to oral sex. A few are even FDA-approved for vaginal use, which also means they're safe to use with condoms.

 Sadie Sez:

Rejuvenate to lubricate. Water-based lubes can lose their slick in the heat of passion. You can either reapply, or use a few drops of saliva or water to quickly reactivate your lube. Try it!

For easy clean-up, choose a colorless formula so it'll wash out of sheets, bedspreads, and any couch where you might get unexpectedly frisky. After sex, just wipe down with a warm washcloth or take a steamy shower.

Silicone-Based Lubes

Why try silicone if water-based lubes work so well? You decide:

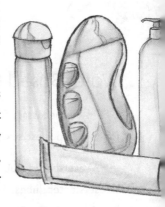

Silicone Pros. More slippery, lasts longer, stays slick in water, doesn't get absorbed into the skin, virtually never dries out in the heat of passion, good for massages, recommended for anal play.

Silicone Cons. Tougher after-sex clean-up, not water-soluble, not recommended for vaginal sex and will "melt" silicone toys.

The rule of thumb? Choose your lube based on how you plan to use it. Silicone is good for anal sex due to its longer lasting consistency, but you'll have to wait till it exits naturally. And it's good for waterplay in the tub or shower, but can make the floor dangerously slippery.

Oil-Based Lubes

Oil-based lubes are created especially for out-of-this-world handjobs and male masturbation only. They're never a wise choice if you're planning to enjoy intercourse—they can promote unpleasant vaginal infections. They're also not condom compatible because they can degrade the latex.

Flavored Lubes

If you like your oral sex a little sweeter, give flavored lubes a swirl. Try the always-popular strawberry, as well as raspberry, kiwi and many others that are more than likable— they're lickable.

Most are water-based and latex-friendly. They'll usually wash right out of the sheets. And the fruity flavor can also help mask scents you may not enjoy, such as latex and rubber from condoms and toys.

> ## Sadie Sez:
>
> **The strawberry penis!** Flavored lubes are perfect for enhancing a guy's scent, which can make going down a lot sweeter.

Which Lube For You?

Women ask me all the time to recommend a long-lasting lube that's safe for the body. I tell them to start with those sample sizes you can pick up for about a buck, or a small bottle—then embark on a "scientific" mission with your guy till you score the loudest *"Ohhh Yessss!!!"* Rate each one for overall lasting time and slickness, resistance to stickiness, and pleasing taste and texture.

I personally wasn't satisfied with the lubes I tried, so I created my own water-based lubes that have everything I was looking for, such as condom-compatibility, FDA-approval and a smooth, no-sticky formula.

Are you among the many women who have a sensitivity to certain ingredients found in lubes, such as Nonoxynol-9 (an ingredient in spermicide), and sugar derivatives? If a lube is irritating you or your partner, discontinue use and look at the ingredient list to see if it contains anything that could be the culprit. Try different lubes until you find the right one for you.

Lube Application & Etiquette

There's an art to applying lube that makes it even sexier. Try this:

Warm it! Lube that sits out on your nightstand might as well have been sitting in your fridge when you apply it directly to hot body parts. The solution? Pour some into your palms first, then rub it around till the friction heats it up. Or place the bottle of lube into a bowl of hot water you've thoughtfully placed at bedside.

Wipe it! What do you do with all that excess lube on your fingers and hands? Wipe it on his back? The dust ruffle? Your peeled-off clothes? Why not just keep a clean towel within arm's reach?

Pour it! How much lube should you use? The rule of thumb is you can never use too much, but if you feel you're not getting enough friction, you may be over-pouring. ♥

Tickle His Pickle

7 Giving Great Hand

M ost guys will tell you that receiving a handjob is one of life's greatest pleasures. But getting one that's truly erotic and exotic is a first-class upgrade to Cloud 9.

Your guy is surely an old hand at satisfying himself. But he'll be the first to admit that *nothing* compares to the thrill of your soft, warm, lubricated digits on his penis. It's the best skin-on-skin pleasure you can give him without thinking about birth control and safer sex. And he'll jump for joy at the chance to skip those sensation-dulling condoms.

Just think of your hands as creative sex toys with lots of moving pleasure parts. And because your fingertips are flush with sensitive nerve endings, you can actually feel his excitement, too. For starters, be sure your fingernails are trimmed smooth and hangnail-free, and your hands are moisturized and naked of all rings and jewelry that can snag and scratch. And if your hands are cold, warm them under running hot water or by tucking them between your thighs.

Imagine. By the time you finish this chapter, you'll know more about pleasuring his penis than he's learned in his entire life!

The Basics

Let's start with a few general pointers:

Rhythm. Good hand technique is like good music. When you find the right rhythm, you're on your way to creating a masterpiece.

Pressure. A feather-touch can be too soft; a firm grip can be too much. But the instant you mimic real vaginal snugness, he'll be putty in your hands. Try inserting a finger or two inside yourself to get a feel for your own snugness. Now you know how tight he may like it.

Angle. Do you only stroke your guy northward toward the belly button, never to points west, or even south? The angle changes the sensation, but be careful: some guys are strictly northerners.

Wetness. While soft, dry teasing can feel good for starters, a handjob really gets going the moment you pour on the slippery lube.

Triggers. No matter how well you master everything else, your big finish will come only when you glide your hand over his trigger points: the ridge, the V-spot and the head.

Listen. Tune in to your guy. His *oohhhs* and *aaaahs* speak volumes—just like his body language. So will his mouth, if you just ask!

 Sadie Sez:

Learn from the master. Who knows better what your guy likes—than your guy? Ask him seductively for a first-hand demonstration. As you watch him show you his favorite techniques, just wrap your hand around his and take it from there.

Tickle His Pickle

Revealing The Prize

Want to tease him mercilessly? Your sexy torture can begin right through his clothes. The light pressure of your fingertips pressing soft cotton against his growing penis will drive him crazy. Just be sure there's expansion room in his pants—it's about to get crowded down there!

Now, for his grand entrance. Reveal his penis slowly, even if you've seen it a million times—he still loves when you first take it out. But be gentle. A scrape against a jagged open zipper can cost him his erection. So can an accidental 'snap' of his briefs' elastic waistband. *Oops!*

Now trace one fingertip up and down the shaft. Or tap and tickle. Or lightly bounce it up and down. Every living cell in his penis is now screaming out for more of your touch.

Get Slippery!

He's past light and teasing. He's ready for hot and heavy. What better time than to bring out the lube?

Lube starter. To use your own natural lube, pool-up some saliva inside your mouth. Now cup your hand over your lips and quietly, gracefully, deposit it onto your fingertips. Then spread it all around the head of his penis for incredible sensations from the first touches of your slippery fingers.

Lube booster. For long-lasting slipperiness, have a good sex lube at-hand. You can drizzle some right onto his penis, or be a considerate lover and warm it up by rubbing it in your palms first.

Head's Up

Just a few more pointers will turn a good handjob into a virtuoso performance:

Sensitive guy? Just like you may be ultra-sensitive to direct clitoral stimulation, he might squirm from over-stimulation of his head. See how he reacts, and if it's over the top, try stroking him just *beneath* the ridge, and see if he wants you to glide over the head when he's about ready to orgasm.

Uncircumcised? Remember that his foreskin is very thin and delicate, so don't slide it down too far, too hard or too fast. You can gently stroke with the foreskin alone, but it's always a good idea to apply lots of lube.

Tuckered out? What if the energy in your hand or wrist is finished before he is? Then switch hands! Or take a break and give him a long, wet, deep kiss—but keep caressing his penis.

Try These Positions

The better you feel, the better he'll feel. Whichever position you choose, just be sure your hands can move freely, and you're comfortable, balanced and warm.

The most common position for a handjob is to lie down right next to him, but these exciting variations will thrill him deeply:

♥ You straddle his legs for bird's eye view—or even wrap your legs around his.

♥ You kneel on the floor while he stands in front of you.

♥ You lie behind him, simulating his own masturbation motions.

♥ He straddles your hips, so he can caress your breasts and enjoy watching you stroke him.

♥ You each sit cross-legged facing the TV, twisting your torsos toward each other. Now watch an adult video while your hands work their magic.

The Grand Finale

His muscles are tensing, his breathing is accelerating, his penis is bulging and his balls are tightening. *This is your cue to keep doing exactly what you're doing—with the same consistent speed, rhythm and pressure. Don't change a thing!*

If he should suddenly veer away from his orgasm, try more stimulation to the head. Or less. Or add some lube. Or just ask him what he'd like you to do.

Tickle His Pickle

When he reaches that tantalizing point-of-no-return, don't stop—ever—even if your wrist feels like it's going to fall off! After the first orgasmic pulsations, begin downshifting your motions, because he's starting to become extra sensitive. *But don't stop—keep stroking slowly and softly until his last orgasmic contraction.*

For a true handjob masterpiece, remember: he LOVES to watch himself come. And he LOVES to watch you watching him. You will launch your guy into seventh heaven by inviting it out of him with hot, spontaneous passion, and then sending it where he can see everything. Right before he explodes, offer him your breasts, tummy, neck, face, arms or even feet for him to come on, and you will be worshiped like never before!

For a graceful finish, never race for the tissues or jump straight into the shower. Tell him how much he turned you on. Caress his penis very gently. Play with his come. Cuddle. Give him a nice deep kiss. Then give him an orgasm aftershock: hold his softening penis at the base, and bring your hand slowly up the shaft, putting light pressure on the underside, like you're squeezing the last bit of toothpaste out of the tube. *Aaaah.*

Sadie Sez:

Do unto others. How do guygasms feel? We'll never know for sure, but it probably feels very similar to our own orgasms. After all, guys have the same ultra-sensitive nerve endings in the head of the penis that we've got in the clitoris. And our bodies react orgasmically in much the same way: involuntary contractions of the PC muscle after that delicious point-of-no-return.

My point? Try the same touching techniques on your guy that you crave yourself: softer rather than harder, slower rather than faster—as well as knowing the moment when faster is better than slower!

Basic Grips

It's easy to get comfortable with just one grip and forget there are many more variations than you even see here. Not every grip will work for your guy—so be sure to improvise—and discover which ones become his new favorites. Don't forget the lube!

oh-Oh-OH-KAY! To form the world's most natural grip, make the "OK" sign by touching your index (or middle) finger to

oh-Oh-OH-KAY!

your thumb, then slip it around his shaft. Now you can travel the entire length, adjusting the pressure to his liking.

Thank U! Cradle his penis in the 'U' between your thumb and your fingers, with your thumb touching the underside of his shaft. Keeping your wrist loose and your grip firm, begin stroking at a diagonal angle.

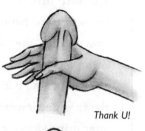

Thank U!

Sausage Wrap. Just enclose his shaft in your five hot little fingers with your thumb at the top and stroke.

Upside-Down Sausage Wrap. Reposition your wrist so your thumb is facing the bottom of his shaft.

Sausage Wrap

Two-Fister. Try any of the basic grips above, but use two hands. Don't lose your balance!

Upside-Down Sausage Wrap

Handjob How-To's

Combine your favorite grips with these erotic techniques and write your own happy endings.

Ol' Faithful. Hold him around the base of his shaft, and as you slowly glide your fingers up over the head of his penis, tighten your grip. Before you head back down, loosen your fingers. Use your other hand to caress his balls or his taint.

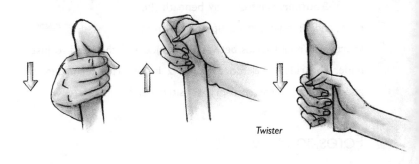

Twister

Twister. With every stroke, give a slippery twist up and down the length of his shaft. Just think of the classic barber shop stripe on the pole!

Pumper. Starting at the base of his penis, stroke way up past the tip. Start again at the base and keep repeating. This big-sensation stroke works well to turn soft into hard.

Pumper

Turtleneck. No lube necessary! Grasp him firmly just under the ridge, and stretch his skin without gliding—up and down in mini-strokes.

Knob Polisher. Place your open palm on top of the head of his penis, enclose him in your fingers, and begin twisting around like you're polishing his knob.

V-Spotter. Start directly beneath the head, and glide your hand up and down in

Knob Polisher

short, swift mini-strokes between the middle of the head to just under the ridge—no more than 1-2 inches. This technique is good if your guy has an overly-sensitive head.

Foreskin How To's

Let's Roll! Gently grip his skin and glide it along his shaft, rolling it over his sensitive head and back down again. Don't over-stroke, use lube, and ask for his feedback.

Mad Hatter. Lube up his head, stretch up his foreskin, and lightly pinch it between your thumb and middle finger. Now roll his foreskin in tiny, gentle circles on his head for a nice scalp rub.

Two-Handed Handjobs

Double Twister. Same as the *Twister*, but use both hands. Now twist together in one direction, then back again. Just glide

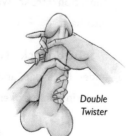

Double Twister

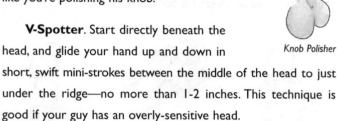

smoothly over his skin. Now try twisting your wrists in opposite directions. But no "rope burns!"

Cigar Roller. With open palms, place each hand on opposite sides of his penis. Slide them up and down, keeping your palms straight and open. Now try rolling them back and forth in opposite directions while you stroke up and down.

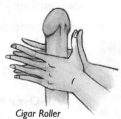

Cigar Roller

Pleasure Tunnel. Do the "OK" sign around the head of his penis, and begin a downward stroke, followed immediately with the same motion from your other hand. Keep repeating from the

Pleasure Tunnel

top. Gradually enlarge your stroking surface by including more fingers, working into the *Sausage Wrap*. Now reverse your direction and add a twist at the head.

Two Thumbs Up. Straddling yourself over his legs, wrap both hands around his shaft, placing the fingerprints from both your thumbs directly on his V-spot. Now massage that V-spot in small circular motions till it stands for Victory!

Two Thumbs Up   73

Three Pointer. With his erection aimed at his bellybutton, keep stroking your open palm up along its underside. If his love juice lands inside his belly button, you get three points!

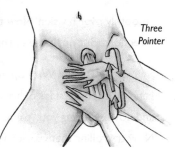

Three Pointer

All-Over Massage. Lube up both your hands completely. Now massage everything, from his belly button down to his inner thighs. As you glide over his skin, begin focusing more and more attention on his penis, balls and taint.

Handjob Extras

All Hands On Dick. Don't forget to bring your other hand into the action. Or one of his. The more the merrier!

Taint It Fine. Press your fingertips, knuckles or a fist gently into his taint. Stroke with your other hand.

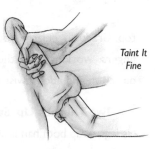

Taint It Fine

Hot Options. Since your mouth and one hand are free, why not put them to good use on his mouth and nipples. Don't forget to caress his balls, taint, butt, inner thighs—or even tug his pubic hair lightly.

Giving Great Hand

Go Underground. Feel his shaft where it goes under his skin by pressing your fingers between his balls, near the top of his scrotum.

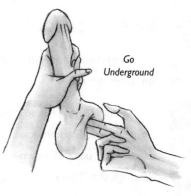

Go Underground

Nail Grazin'. A light, light scratch can really get him going. Gently glide your nails along his shaft, inner thighs and balls.

Spread 'Em. His orgasm will take on a different feeling if you have him open his legs wide while you're giving him your handjob.

Human Penis Ring. While you're stroking him with one hand, grasp him tightly at the base with your thumb and middle finger of the other. This will keep the blood in his penis and give him explosive orgasms.

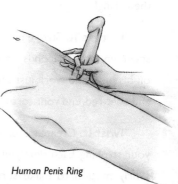

Human Penis Ring

Double His Pleasure. Holding his penis like the *Human Penis Ring*, use your leading hand to stroke and twist at the top. When he reaches the point-of-no-return, bring your other hand up and surprise him with a double grand finish.

Try A SpiceJob!

Sometimes those little extras are just what's needed to put him over the top.

Wrist It. Just like in golf, your wrist action can change the entire stroke. Slacken your wrist and let your fingers follow as you stroke up and down—or you can stiffen up your wrist, although that'll be more tiring on your arm.

Tease It. Just before he explodes, divert your attention away from his penis to his other erogenous zones. Then start up on his penis again. Repeat. By the time he comes, he'll be on the ceiling!

Torture It. Stroke him slowly for a couple of minutes, then speed up for 10 seconds. As soon as he's ready to explode, back off his head and work just the shaft. You'll see him get rock-hard and beet-red. End your torture session with his favorite technique.

Twist It. Create a slippery twisting rhythm to go along with your stroking. Each time you reach the head, add in a little extra swirly motion to make sure you light up every single nerve ending he's got.

Tap It. Light tapping up and down his penis—and on his V-spot—will drive him insane, or wake up a penis that's playing hard to get.

Look Ma…No Hands!

Violin Concerto. Run the soft skin of your arm up and down along his shaft, V-spot and ridge, like you're playing soft classical music in an orchestra.

Lip Job. Slather your vulva with plenty of lube, then position yourself on top, with his penis snuggly between your labia. Now glide the two of you into heaven!

Leave It To Cleavage. No guy can resist the space between the breasts. Just lube 'em up, push 'em together, and slide him in. ♥

Leave It To Cleavage

8 Giving Great Head

I f there's a heaven, what do you suppose guys are praying for when they arrive? Hot fudge sundaes? You bet—being licked off them by eager, creative, bodacious angels!

Blowjobs. Head. Hummers. BJs. Going Down. Fellatio. Whatever you call it, guys will do anything to get it. After all, it's their complete erotic fantasy come true: sights, sounds, sensations and screaming orgasms. Oral sex is as hot and intimate as it comes.

That explains why many guys dream about the female mouth even more than the vagina (if you can believe that!). Why? Both are warm, wet and tight—but the mouth has a tongue that licks, lips that suck, and teeth that tease.

So be empowered! You have his full trust. He's at your mercy. And you control every moment of his pleasure. Oral sex is the ultimate sexual gift you can give to your guy. So why not give it your all?

Blowjob Basics

Did you find the pamphlet that came with the guy's penis the first time you tried oral sex? *No?* Then I'll bet you had to figure it all out all by yourself, while you awkwardly took his manhood into your mouth.

So let's start fresh today, okay?

I'm about to show you enticing oral sex techniques for you to take only as far as you please. You don't have to "deep throat"

Giving Great Head

him. You don't have to taste his come. And you certainly don't have to swallow—although you just might like it after all. Just pick and choose what tickles your fancy, and advance from there.

Start by getting comfortable. Oral sex can be a bit tiring, so be sure to position yourself so your upper body and shoulders can move up and down with you. And if your neck gets sore, he's got two hands that should be more than willing to massage it for you.

Sadie Sez:

The best blowjob ever! Do you know the ONE technique that elevates a great blowjob into an outstanding blowjob? **Enthusiasm**. More than paint-by-the-numbers know-how, true oral sex artistry comes from wrapping energy, emotion, joy and rapture into your orgasmic masterpiece. Try it!

You'll also discover that if you're currently pregnant, or you don't want to be, oral sex is the perfect pleasure solution! And if either of you has a physical disability or recent injury that makes intercourse challenging or impossible, a good blowjob will have you both feeling better fast.

As for you, just remember: you set the depth. You set the pace. You set your comfort. You're in control.

Safer Sex Precaution: To fully enjoy the pleasures of oral sex, both of you should be totally monogamous and free of all sexually transmitted diseases (STDs). If you are not monogamous lovers, or either of you engages in any high-risk behavior, read the Appendix at the end of this book <u>before</u> trying any of these techniques to learn how safer sex will maximize your pleasure while minimizing your risk.

Ready...Set...Blow!

Set out just a few props now and be ready for all the action to come.

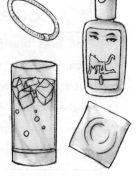

♥ **Hair Band.** If you're done with messy hair fun, you'll want to tie your hair back to give him a better view and keep those strands from dropping into your mouth in the heat of passion.

- ♥ **Thirst Quenchers.** Set out a glass of water, seedless grapes or even a few mints or menthol cough drops to keep your lips and mouth wet and lubricated.

- ♥ **Slippery Stuff.** Buy some good fruit-flavored water-based lickable lube—and place it within arm's reach.

- ♥ **Protection.** For safer sex, have an ample supply of latex condoms close by.

You're ready…now let's explore the four phases of oral sex.

Phase I: The Agony Of Anticipation

Start by filling his senses with your feminine mystique. Put on that sensuous perfume you know he likes. Spray the sheets with lavender. Wear something new and sexy.

Now whisper in his ear exactly what you've been fantasizing about all day—and how you're about to share that fantasy with him. Model and pose in your sexy outfit for him, while you touch yourself with sensual squeezes and exotic strokes. Tell him that what you are about to do together really turns you on, and let him tell you what he wants you to do, too.

Land soft, wet kisses on his mouth, neck and earlobes. Show him what foreplay is all about! Warm up your mouth on his

finger—or your own—so he can start imagining your mouth on his penis. Let him hear what your sucking sounds like.

Now bring your mouth down just far enough on his body so he'll think *maybe, hopefully, possibly* you'll keep on going. Pause at his belly button long enough to heat up his brainwaves with loud silent pleading, before you continue your quest southward.

Unzip his pants and begin teasing his penis lightly with your hand as you sweep your mouth around his belly button, hips, thighs—in other words, everywhere *but.* Now lightly press your puckered lips onto his penis right through his underwear. Blow some warm moist air. Nibble lightly. Glide your talented lips up and down his shaft.

Phase II: Peeling & Revealing

It's time for the clothes to start disappearing. Look up at him, gaze into his bedazzled eyes, and trace the tip of your tongue slowly, sensually along your warm, moist lips. Then gently pull down his underwear so you reveal only the head of his penis. Hold onto the elastic band as you let your soft cheeks brush up against his head, so he'll scream silently, "Just suck it already!!!"

Now guide his penis to your mouth, and tease him with a couple of kisses before you remove every trace of clothing and move in for a closer lick.

Reach down and touch yourself, letting your fingers get wet with your own love juice. Then put them in your mouth or offer him your glistening fingers to lick. Look him in the eye—show him how turned on you are. You'll surely see how turned on he is!

Now you may begin to notice a few "love drops" appear at the tip. It's an excellent lubricant, so spread it all around his head and ridge and continue your teasing.

The first touches of your mouth will give him the most incredible sensations. Ever so slowly, glide the tip of your tongue up over the head, down the shaft and back up again. Stay slow, even though he'll be begging you to go faster. Now take his whole head into your mouth for one full suck, and let it pop out with one loud sexy "slurp."

Phase III: Head-On Head

You're now into the faster, rhythmical phase he's been aching for. So get comfortable—it's going to get wild! Try the

Sadie Sez:

Illuminate yourself. Don't hide under the covers, or let your long hair block his visual treat. From room light to candlelight, set the glow so he can see. Are you brave enough to do this in broad daylight?

techniques you'll find on the following pages as your starting point, and improvise from there. Be sure to include these BJ-boosters, too:

♥ You only need to put his penis into your mouth as far as you feel comfortable. You can start shallow, and increase the depth slowly.

♥ No need to limit yourself to one technique—try three or more in the same session, along with different speeds, pressures, grips and motions. Slow down, speed up. Keep him guessing what's next.

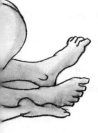

♥ Pay attention to what's going on inside your mouth. Make sure it's always nice 'n slippery, keep your teeth out of the way, run his head along the roof of your mouth for a bumpy ridge effect, lick the tip of his head while it's inside and swirl on it with your tongue.

♥ Look at him seductively through your hanging hair. Later, tie it back so he can see you. Or ask him to hold it for you. Look up into his eyes while you're pleasing him, grin seductively and whisper, "Do you like that, baby?"

♥ If you get dry, sip more water, or just drizzle on more flavored lube. Don't be shy—make a sexy production out if it.

♥ At least once or twice, take his penis out of your mouth and admire it. Tell him how good it feels and that you love doing this for him. Keep stroking with your hand when your mouth is on a break.

♥ Every 7-to-10 strokes, glide your mouth all the way up, over and off his head, pause-to-tease, then take it in your mouth again and go back down.

♥ Be noisy. He loves the sounds of sucking, ooohing and aaah-ing, as well as the vibrations of you humming.

♥ Most every guy loves to watch his woman self-pleasure right in front of him, and he loves it even more when he doesn't have to ask!

Giving Great Head

♥ Remember: use teeth softly (or ask if he likes nibbling —and how hard.)

♥ Reach up and hold his hand for added intimacy and connection. Squeeze your palms together for several moments. Then put your fingers in his mouth so he can suck, too. Ask him to demonstrate on your fingers what he'd like you to do to him.

♥ Bring his balls into play. Lube them up and caress them gently for the full erotic experience. Lightly tug, squeeze and roll them around in the cup of your hand. Then move on to his taint and butt.

♥ Now break out the vibrators! Give him the wonderful sensation of vibrations along with the soft warm feel of your mouth.

♥ Take your time. Remember, enthusiasm is key. Love what you're doing!

 Sadie Sez:

Live a fantasy of your own! Fulfill YOUR fantasy of being with two men! Have him use your favorite dildo on you while you're going down on him.

Phase IV: The Eruption

It's time to reap the reward for your loving caresses and erotic inspiration.

The key to his climax will come from your steady application of the one Golden Technique that works for your guy. Once you discover it, store it away in your memory and you'll enjoy many happy endings together.

When do you begin the Golden Technique? When you sense he's getting close to orgasming: faster breathing, louder moaning, tensing muscles, and gasping, "Oh yeah right THERE!!!" Just stay on your Golden Technique with the same speed, rhythm and pressure—*and don't stop!* Then when he erupts:

Hand Finish. If you're not ready to taste him, substitute your hand for your mouth without missing a beat. Use one of the techniques in Chapter 7 as you get more comfortable with the feel of his penis and his orgasm. If you're not sure when he's about to come, ask him to tell you.

Lip Finish. With your lips over his head, press your tongue against his peehole. As you stroke him with your hand, let his spurts ricochet left and right off your tongue. You can easily push his love juice out of your mouth, letting it seep down his shaft. He will feel great—and it won't hit the back of your throat.

Mouth Finish. If you're ready for him to come inside your mouth, but you don't want to swallow, try this: aim him toward the inside of your cheek and use the back of your tongue to close off your throat. Then try swallowing a little, or let it all seep out onto his penis in one glorious finish.

Post Eruption. Use this serene time to whisper, "did you enjoy that?" Very gently fondle his penis as you tell him how turned on you are, how good he feels when he comes, how you love the sight of his penis, hard or soft, and why he's the most delicious thing on this planet.

He will now be very sensitive around the head, although he'll enjoy your tender kisses beneath it, and the feeling of his penis softening in the warmth of your mouth—as long as you don't brush your tongue against his now ultra-sensitive head. If you're up for it, sweetly and slowly lick up some of his come. Watching you will be very exciting for him.

And while he'll gladly kiss the ground you walk on, he may or may not be too eager to kiss you till you've wiped off your mouth. Ask—he'll tell you.

To Swallow Or Not To Swallow

That is the question, right?

Whether you choose to swallow, or let him come everywhere with great abandon, remember that he LOVES watching you receive his come like sweet nectar.

Swallow Not. It's entirely up to you, because there are plenty of ways to enjoy his milky shower. It's okay to say, 'I don't feel comfortable swallowing, but I'd love you come on my breasts…stomach…neck…face…anywhere!'

As he's coming, gaze into his eyes and tell him how he turns you on. While his body lives out its orgasm, there's no better sight or sound for him to behold.

Wherever it goes, it will get messy, and messy is good, so welcome the mess—or spread a towel on the bed to save the sheets. And if he wore a condom, the mess is completely self-contained!

Swallow Yes. You're about to offer your guy one of the greatest gifts a woman can bestow upon her man. To receive his orgasm, part your lips like you're drinking water from a fountain, place them snuggly over his head, and swallow as he comes. You may find it easier to take his head inside and aim him toward your cheek. Or just take him in as far as you can and go for it!

You may need to practice your technique so you don't gag. Always avoid making jarring spitting noises—just let it flow out of your mouth if you like. And never stop your hand or mouth from moving as he comes—his climax depends on it!

 Sadie Sez:

Come...the low carb treat! Sure it's creamy, but come is low in fat, low in calories, low in carbohydrates and high in quality protein. It's also got a bit of zinc, calcium, magnesium, vitamins C and B12, potassium, phosphorus and fructose, along with a healthy portion of DNA.

Conquering Those *What If's*

What if I don't like giving oral sex?

Are you flashing back to a bad experience? An ex who demanded it? Feelings of shame or guilt? Questions of respect? Perhaps you've worked through your issues, or now have a greater sexual maturity. Be honest with your partner. And if you're ready to try again, start with little licks and nibbles, going only as far as you're comfortable, trying a little more each time.

What if he doesn't smell good?

Haul him into the shower and give him an good erotic soap-down, followed by a hot waterfall blowjob. Offer to groom and shave his pubic hair, too.

What if I'm practicing safe sex?

You don't have to give up oral sex to practice safer sex. Unless you're in a monogamous relationship and are certain both of you are free of all hidden risks, see the Appendix for safer sex tips and information on condoms.

What if he shoves my head down?

He just needs a little training. Take his hands off your head, and in a loving way, place them elsewhere.

If the head pushing starts again, stop and tell him nicely that it makes you uncomfortable. If he persists, you can just stop. Game over. Be sure to bring it up when you're not in the heat of passion. Or next time, tie his hands to the bed!

What if I gag?

Everyone gags. It's your body's involuntary reaction to something blocking your throat, and it can save your life if you're choking.

If you discover you're gagging, just stroke him with your hand till the feeling settles down. You can whisper "Oops…you're just so big," followed up with a sassy smile and wet lick on his tender-spot.

Here's how to short-circuit gagging: wrap your hands around the base of his penis, creating a buffer so *you* determine how deeply you'll let his penis into your mouth—no matter how much he thrusts. And make sure your lips and mouth are extra wet.

As you get comfortable, loosen your buffer a little to take more of him in. Relax your throat. Choose a position that matches the curve of his penis to the curve of your throat, so he's not aiming directly at your gag spot. Or try a numbing gel, which you apply near the back of your throat to temporarily reduce the gag reflex. And more importantly, don't try this after a full meal!

Remember: it'll take some practice and patience. In the meantime, he'll be perfectly happy with you focusing on the top half of his penis!

What if he wants me to swallow?

It's entirely up to you. Swallow only if you're comfortable.

What if I don't like the taste?

If you're recalling a bad taste from a past experience, you may be pleasantly surprised to know genetics, diet and time between orgasms can affect flavor, texture and force. So while your ex may have tasted like bleach, alfalfa sprouts, brie cheese or salty milk, your beau could taste like kiwi.

You can sweeten him up by feeding him strawberries, melon, kiwi and pineapples the day before, and cutting out the red meat, alcohol and cigarettes. Or just cover his penis with chocolate syrup, canned fruits, whipped cream or honey to mask the flavor.

What if he's pierced?

If he was pierced recently, make sure he's completely healed before you engage in oral sex. After that, his penis may become more sensitive—or too sensitive—around the site of the piercing. Communication and experimentation are the keys. And be careful about chipping your teeth, or simply ask him to remove the barbell till you're done.

What if I'M pierced?

Here's a trick for you: freeze a barbell tongue piece, then put it in your tongue. Now take a mouthful of hot tea and go down on him. He'll feel the sensations of both hot and cold simultaneously! Now rub the frozen piece down the shaft past his tender-spot, down his ball seam and to his taint.

What if he's **HUGE**?

A guy who's well-hung is more than proud—he also understands the challenge you face. Relax. Get comfortable. Use lots of saliva, water and lube. And stay balanced—you're going to need both hands to use as an extension of your mouth.

What if I get a jaw cramp?

Just like a runner holds back a burst of energy for the finish line, so should you. Pace yourself. Substitute your hand when your mouth gets tired. Lean on pillows for comfort. If you start to cramp, change your position, or stimulate him elsewhere and return to his penis when you're refreshed. Or just take a breather for a sip of water as you look into his eyes and lick your luscious lips.

 ## Sadie Sez:

Be a show-off! The best blowjobs include incredible visuals. Try to position yourself where he can clearly see as much of you as he can take in. Arch your back and put your butt up in the air!

First Licks

Ready? Let's start with the basics.

Lip Gloss. Flood your puckered lips with saliva, then glide them gently up and down and all around his shaft. Swirl around the head, too.

Gummer. Curl back your moistened lips over your front teeth. Not only does it feel good, but your lips will protect him from bumping into your teeth.

Lip Gloss

Tip Top. Slide the tip of your wet tongue all around his head, peehole and V-spot. Work your tongue into every crevice and skin fold till he's taut and hard.

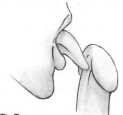

Tip Top

All-Day Sucker. Push your lips outward and create a gentle suction on his shaft. Now suck 'n glide up and down without losing the vacuum.

Laplander. With your tongue full, wide and relaxed, lick his penis upward like a melting ice cream cone.

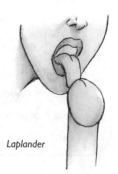

Laplander

Skin Flicks. Flutter and flick the tip of your hot wet tongue from the top of his penis all the way to the bottom of his balls.

Skin Flicks

 Sadie Sez:

Liquidate yourself. With your mouth around his erect penis, take him in as deeply as you can. You'll find that the deeper you let him probe, the more your brain will naturally trigger a stream of luscious liquid in your mouth—and even down south!

The Classic Blowjob

Timeless. Legendary. Craved. Go for it!

Step 1: Form the "OK" sign with your thumb and forefinger. Place it over your lips.

Step 2: Gracefully bring your face down over his penis while you form the *Sausage Grip* with your hand. Now allow him to glide up through the bottom of your lightly held fist.

The Classic Blowjob

Step 3: Continue south until his head comes through the top of your fist and into your mouth. As you take him in, begin the *Twister* technique with your hand, first on the upstroke, then on the downstroke.

Step 4: Bring everything into perfect synch. Coordinate your favorite combo of hand grips and stroking with your glorious wet lips around his penis.

Exotic Variations

Start with *The Classic Blowjob*, then try one of these variations as your springboard to wild improvisations. Which of these will become your one Golden Technique to finish him off?

102

Flick Off. With his head in your mouth, flick or roll your tongue around the top. Try flattening your tongue to create more surface area.

Flick On. Alternate suction with flicking in the technique above.

Fruit Juicer. Twist your neck left and right so it feels like your mouth is swiveling on his penis as you go up and down. Add in the *Flick Off* and listen to him moan.

Suction Seduction. Suck on his shaft to hold the skin tight to your lips, and work your magic up and down his penis. Add in a twisting motion without breaking the seal.

Tea Bagging. Let your tongue roam down beyond his shaft and onto his balls. Tap them lightly with your tongue, increasing the intensity. Now gently fill your mouth with one (or both!) of them.

Tea Bagging   103

Sadie Sez:

Rocket his missile. Grab a Missile popsicle out of the freezer and give your guy a visual demonstration of what you're planning to do to him. Then hand it to him to eat as you head south!

Sweet Nothings. As softly and lightly as you possibly can, tease the head of his penis with your mouth and tongue. Let him feel mostly your hot moist breath.

Hummer. Place your puckered lips on him and hum *"The Star Spangled Banner."* The vibrations should make him stand and salute!

Yummer. Add some chocolate syrup, whipped cream or mashed strawberries and eat him clean.

V-Spotting. Work the V-spot with the tip of your tongue, flicking and licking. Now open your mouth, extend your tongue, and let *him* rub his V-spot along its long, wet, luxurious surface.

XXX-treme. Change the temperature in your mouth and change the sensation around his penis. Fill your mouth with ice water, hot tea or shaved ice—and plunge him in. Or just blow your cool or hot breath over his eager penis.

Ivory Hunt. Break the no-teeth rule—gently! Glide your teeth down the length of his shaft, or run the head of his penis over the broad-surfaced molars in the back of your mouth—*with a feather-light touch!*

Waterfall. Place a cup of hot water or tea beside the bed, and when he's not looking, fill your mouth with the hot liquid. Now go down on him and let the hot water spill out of your mouth for a hot, wet, slippery experience! Alternate with ice cubes and cool water.

Say When. Slowly run your finger up the underside of his penis. Tell him to say "There!" when you reach the most sensitive spot. Now make love to that spot by licking, nibbling and teasing.

The Skimmer. Take his head into your mouth, barely pressing your lips into his skin. Try this a few times till he becomes a bucking bronco!

Peek-a-Boo. Gently stretch his lubed foreskin down, exposing his sensitive head and shaft to lick with your tongue and to stroke with your fingers. Use the classic "OK" grip.

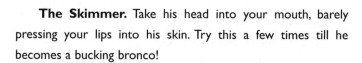

Rocket Boosters

Bait & Switch. Lead him to think you're going to get him off with a handjob, and right before he comes, land your hot mouth on him. For contrast, try a fast hand motion, then a slow, hard suck. Or pull out a vibrator and get shaking!

LipFlip. Lead him to think you're going to get him off with a blowjob, running your lips up and down his shaft till he nearly comes. Then straddle him, and glide your wet vaginal lips up and down along his shaft.

Tricky Dick. With you on your knees, and him dangling his erect penis over you, try bobbing for it without using your hands. Add to the challenge by having him flex his PC muscles to make his penis a moving target. As long as you're down there, go ahead and lick his balls, too.

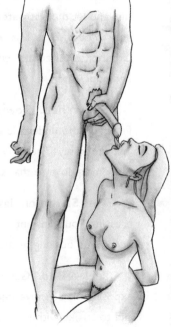

Growth Spurt. Before he's hard, take his entire penis into your mouth and wrap your luscious lips around the base. Feel him start to grow as you work your tongue magic on him, and just move back as he gets bigger.

Tricky Dick

Just Say O. Keep your head still as he does all the thrusting motion into your mouth. You may want to grip your hand around the base or use a penis sleeve to act as a buffer, so he doesn't go too deep.

Just Say O

Vibe Him. Place a cylindrical vibrator over his balls, or whichever part of his manhood is not in your mouth! Then alternate your tongue and a vibe on his penis.

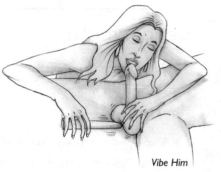

Vibe Him

Ball Buzzer. Place a wireless vibrating cock ring around the base of his shaft, with the vibrator turned towards the bottom, so it presses right into his balls. Now lick and suck while the vibrations put him in orbit.

Ball Buzzer

Penis Alarm Clock. Place a strong mint or menthol cough drop in your mouth—along with his penis. The minty or menthol sensation can awaken the nerve endings even more.

I wanna hold your gland. Men LOVE having their penises touched, licked, rubbed, fondled, tugged, squeezed, blown on and talked to. Try sleeping with it in your hand!

Deep Throating

Some women can take in an entire penis without gagging. Others can do it with practice. But you? Would you? Could you? Here's how:

♥ Since you're actually "swallowing" him—both of you must align the curve of his shaft to the curve of your throat.

♥ His penis will seal off your windpipe, so you won't be able to breathe. No inhaling or exhaling when he's in deep. Take your breaths on the out-strokes.

♥ Lie on your back, and tilt your head down off the edge of the bed. This will open your throat and reduce your impulse to gag.

Giving Great Head

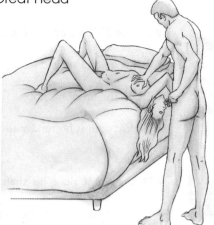

- ♥ Gagging will be part of it. The better you get at deep-throating, the less you'll gag.

- ♥ You are in charge. Always. Vocalize your boundaries and take it at *your* pace. If you're not comfortable, don't do it.

- ♥ If you can't keep up the pace, just deep throat him once in a while during your oral extravaganza. He'll be thrilled!

Sex Gadgets

If your guy is a gadget-lover, he'll flip when you unwrap a sex toy you've selected just for him—or for both of you!

These add-ons for hand- and blowjobs boost the sensations from your fingers, tongue and lips. The choices today are limited only by your own imagination.

Vibrators. I've yet to meet a guy who didn't like the feeling of a vibrator at the base of his shaft or under his balls. Just pick up a little love egg ("bullet") or cylindrical

Cylindrical Vibe

vibe and load it up with batteries. Then try these tricks:

♥ Run it on and around his nipples during your blowjob.

♥ Tickle the tip of his nose.

♥ Glide it against his tender-spot, balls and taint while you kiss his penis.

♥ Lightly run it along his shaft, from tip to bottom.

♥ Gently touch it to the head of his penis for only a moment.

♥ Use it interchangeably with your mouth and hand.

♥ Place a love egg against your cheek while you give him head.

♥ Run it along his taint and butthole. Use lots of lube.

♥ Pick up two: let him play with one on you, too!

Penis Rings. These gadgets wrap tightly around the base of his penis to help him maintain a harder, longer-lasting erection. They'll even give him a more intense orgasm, too. Try one that vibrates!

Note: Rings have a pleasure limit. Play it safe, and don't let him wear it longer than 30 minutes at a time.

Penis Sleeves. For a refreshing change of pace, wrap him in a penis sleeve and glide this lifelike material up and down his shaft. *Tip:* If he's extra large, you can use one as a safety guard to keep his penis from going too far down your throat.

Oral Vibrators. What will they think of next? These tiny micro-vibrators attach to your tongue and vibrate the tip as you work your magic.

Penis Sleeve

Dildos. For backdoor play, just find the one that fits him best. And with so many materials to choose from—latex, silicone, plastic, glass—as well as hundreds of shapes and sizes, you'll have fun just shopping! See Chapter 9 for more information on backdoor pleasure.

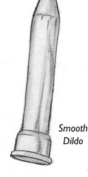

Smooth Dildo

Edibles. Shape a piece of licorice over your teeth to blunt the sharp edges, and then go wild! It feels good to him, and it's tasty for you. Or cover him in fruit-flavored lube and have a party! ❤

9 His Back Door (& More!)

It's surprising how so many totally heterosexual guys will get squeamish if you even *hint* you'd like to try buttplay on them—especially since they're always so gung-ho to do it to you!

Yet anal sex is now more popular than ever among straight men and women today.

If you'd like to try it, you'll find everything you need in this chapter to get started—safely and securely. And the best way to start may be to calm his biggest fears:

"I tried it once and it didn't feel good." (It's all about technique, lover.)

"It's an exit, not an entrance." (It can be both, safely and pleasurably.)

"It's for gay men." (Not when he's naked with a ravishing woman like you!)

Do you know what convinces more and more hetero couples to explore the pleasures of buttplay? Is it intimacy? Passion? Curiosity? Excitement? More exotic, erotic orgasms? Actually, it's all of the above.

Some guys love to be touched down there. Some like to be penetrated down there. And others want you to stay the heck away—although it helps to reassure them this doesn't make them the least bit homosexual: every guy has a prostate, ready to provide many highly pleasurable, direct stimulation orgasms.

You can initiate buttplay by expressing your desires to your guy. But as always, be sure to respect his wishes. If he's still not interested—even after you've enlightened him—that's okay, too. And since this is one area where you can know exactly how your own touch feels, why not pleasure *yourself* there first to see how you like it!

Safer Sex Precaution: To fully enjoy the pleasures of buttplay, both of you should be totally monogamous and free of all sexually transmitted diseases (STDs). If you are recent lovers, or either of you engages in any high-risk behavior, read the tips in this chapter and the Appendix at the end of this book <u>before</u> trying any of these techniques to learn how safer sex will maximize your pleasure while minimizing your risk.

Magic Butt Tour

His Anus & Rectum

His *anus* ("butthole") is the opening at the outermost edge of his anal canal. It's loaded with nerve endings that make it ultra-sensitive to finger, tongue or vibrator stimulation. Even if you've never included his anus in your lovemaking, it joins in anyway, becoming incredibly sensitive when he gets excited, pulsating wildly every time he orgasms. But he's never fully aware of these erotic pulsations until it's being touched—so touch it!

Just inside his anus are two circular muscles called *sphincters*, designed to expand and contract. Even further inside, you'll find the *rectum*, which delivers delightful sensations of pressure, but has very little sensitivity to touch (much the same as the inside of your vagina). To him, these rectal feelings of pressure and fullness may feel at first like he's about to have a bowel movement, but assure him there's nothing to worry about—it's a passageway, not a storage area.

The Prostate

Your guy has a G-spot—although it's not the same as yours. It's the *prostate*, also known as the "P-spot"—and you can find it a few inches inside his anus.

The prostate creates and stores the ejaculatory fluid that ultimately carries his sperm to you. Since massaging the prostate can make his orgasms feel more amazing than ever, it's worth feeling your guy out to see if he wants to be felt out.

The prostate is easy to find with a well-lubed index or middle finger. He may actually come from your finger action alone—but it usually takes lots of practice receiving prostate stimulation simultaneously with your hand- and blowjobs.

If he loses his erection while you're rubbing his prostate, don't worry—it happens to some guys. Just start him off inside, and finish him off outside. And when you're done, be sure to remove your finger gently—and slowly.

Sadie Sez:

Play nurse! Perhaps a little "professional" play-acting will get him into the mood for buttplay. Tell him you're a nurse, and you need to examine his buttocks. Have him lay down on his stomach as you begin your "exam." Start with a light butt massage, and say that you need to go in deeper. Bring out your "instrument"—a finger or mini-vibrator—and complete your exam!

Prostate Massage—
From The Outside-In

If he's not yet relaxed enough to desire your finger inside, you can still caress his P-spot from the outside.

While you're engaged in hot oral activity, run your lubed fingers down behind his scrotum onto his taint. Your teasing fingertips will feel extraordinary, but as soon as you increase the pressure, you can indirectly stimulate his prostate.

Vary the sensations with firmer pressures and circular strokes, together with your hand- or blowjob, and you'll give him a truly *amazing* orgasm. You'll also awaken the nerve endings at the opening of his anus. Will this tempt him to try finger buttplay next time?

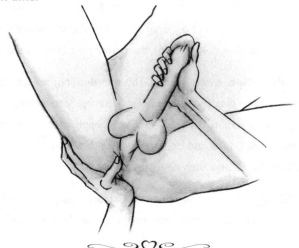

The Rules To Buttplay

When unlocking his backdoor, keep these keys in mind:

Cleanliness. Good hygiene creates a more comfortable experience. Have him wash up with a hot shower or bath, and suggest he "go" an hour or two beforehand.

Communication. Comfort begins with trust, and trust starts with good communication. If you both agree to go really slowly and to communicate openly and honestly through the entire experience—you'll be just fine.

Relaxation. Prepare him for pleasure by massaging his inner butt-cheeks and inner thighs. This helps get his blood flowing into the area and relaxes his body and butt muscles (a little spanking will help, too!). The best primer for buttplay is sex—so enjoy a hot first round of orgasms before heading to the backside. Remember: the more he relaxes, the better your buttplay can be.

Lubrication. *Always use lube.* The anus does not self-lubricate enough for anal play, and dryness can cause injury to delicate anal and rectal tissue. So B.Y.O.L.—and keep applying it generously. Choose a good lube and be sure to keep it within close reach. *Caution: lube is absolutely necessary during buttplay.*

Safety. Wash hands with anti-bacterial soap, take off all rings, and be sure nails are smoothly filed—no hangnails!

Examine all sex toys to be sure there are no sharp edges—especially on plastic toys that sometimes have rough seams. Just file them down with an emery board.

Ease into it. Start slowly and gradually: your timing, mood, space and vibe need to be just right. Start with simple pleasures, such as massaging only the butt and anus. Then slowly move on to rimming and other exterior techniques.

Easing inside. The anal canal curves toward the front of the body, so your fingers and toys should be flexible enough to curve with it. Go sloooowly when entering and never pull out quickly. Be gentle, and always use lots of lube.

No double-dipping. Be extra careful not to transfer bacteria from the anus to any other parts of the body. Whether you're inserting a tongue, toy or finger into the anus, don't insert them into any other orifice—yours or his—till they're washed and clean.

Orgasmic synergy. Most men and women require direct genital stimulation to orgasm—few people have orgasms by anal stimulation alone. So be sure to add in other pleasures simultaneously—like the awesome hand- and blowjobs you're now even better at!

Take your time. This is an adventure—be patient and don't rush. Your guy may need extra time to get used to it. So go slow and enjoy it!

Buttplay Positions

Try them all till you find your favorites! Here are a few to get you started:

♥ With your guy on his back, sit between his legs so he can see you.

♥ Lay him face-down on the bed, and place pillows under his hips.

♥ Lay him on his side in spoon position, with you behind.

♥ Get behind him while he's on all fours. Now drop his shoulders to the bed.

♥ Try 69, with him on top.

The Buttplay Blastoff

How far in will he like it? Take it one level at a time:

Level 1: Orbiting His Anus—Land Massage

During one of your best blowjobs, pause and seductively whisper, "Do you want me to rock your world like never before?" When he gasps *"YES!"* slowly slip your lubed fingers onto his taint and begin massaging. Before you resume your world-class blowjob, say, "It would make me so hot to play around back here."

No objections? Then begin seducing his anus by running your fingers all around the area, slowly circling his anus. Lightly press one lubed fingertip onto his anus, while you continue pleasuring his penis. Then rub in circular motions, slowly brushing your finger around its outer edges, then rock back and forth in the center. *Ohhhh…*does that feel good!

Level 2: **Probing Inner Space— Galactic Finger Play**

Did your soft, warm fingertip drive him crazy? Would a little more of your finger drive him even crazier? Then try this…

With your hot breath on his excited penis, and your lubed fingertip nestled against his anus, ask him seductively if he'd like a little more of you inside. *No?* Then you've found his limit. *Yes?* Suggest he relax all around your fingertip. When you feel his anus slacken, your lubed finger will seem to slip magically inside his sensitive canal all by itself.

Sadie Sez:

Buttplay boosters. Always stimulate his penis with a primo hand- or blowjob while you're playing with his butt. It'll make the whole experience feel better, as you blend the euphoric sensations of buttplay with the erotic sensations of the blowjob. If he was apprehensive about it beforehand, this will help calm his fears.

Once you're inside about an inch, stay perfectly still so he can get used to this new erotic sensation. Keep stroking his penis. Then, ever so slowly, move in a little further, curving your finger with the natural curve of his canal, and begin in-'n-out

pleasure. Remember: play with his penis at all times during buttplay. Proceed with your first-class blowjob, or switch to a primo handjob!

Level 3: **Planet P-Spot—Warp Drive**

Now he's ready for the best in buttplay. *Slowly* begin searching with your index finger, fingerprint side-up, a little further into his anus along the upper wall. As soon as your knuckle disappears inside, start feeling around for a firm, round bulb that feels like the end of your nose—that's his prostate!

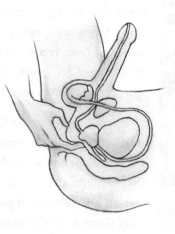

Now start making slow, gentle come hither-type curling motions with your finger—just like you're ticking him under his chin. Then focus on his reactions, and ask whether the motion would feel better harder, softer, faster or slower. You'll know you've got it right when his legs spread wider, his breathing gets faster, he's riding your finger—and if he's a vocal guy, he starts vocalizing.

Rimming

What happens when he feels the sensation of the tip of your tongue on the rim of his anus? Nirvana!

After plenty of heated foreplay, slide your tongue in between his butt-cheeks and get creative! Ravish him by going round 'n round, and keep stimulating him by flicking soft and slow, or lick him with your full-on tongue. Try slight probing with the very tip, pressing into him like you're ringing a doorbell. Don't forget to pleasure him with your hand, too. For a real thrill, spread his cheeks wide apart for uninhibited access.

Here's how to perform world-class analingus with all the sensations and none of the risk! Slip into the kitchen and tear off a large piece of plastic wrap. Generously lube up his anus, and place the wrap across his bottom, pressing a single layer into his crevice. Now let your tongue roam free. If you don't care for the non-taste of the wrap, you can coat the tongue side with something tastier, like fruit-flavored lube. You can also use dental dams (see Appendix).

Butt Pleasure Toys

In addition to tried-and-true dildos and vibrators, consider these other terrific toys designed especially for the butt. They come in tiny shapes and sizes (even a lifelike finger), all the way to XXX-large! Start small, and move up in size over time.

Caution: Any toy you insert into his butt should have a long handle or a flared base, so it doesn't get sucked inside where you can't easily get it out.

Plugs

Put 'em in—and leave 'em in. Butt plugs all have a similar shape—narrow at the base, thickest in the middle, and narrowest on top. The flared base prevents the plug from sliding up inside and disappearing.

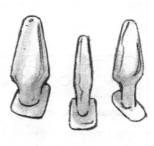

Designed to stay still inside (rather than be pushed in and out), butt plugs do more than give a feeling of fullness while they condition the anus for more fun—they also intensify his sensations at the moment of orgasm.

Tip: To relax his anus for easier insertion, try a vibrating butt plug. Then hand him the remote so he can control the vibration speed—just like he controls the TV clicker!

Beads

Many men and women enjoy the feeling of the anus opening and closing around these smooth orgasm-enhancing beads. Just pre-insert a strand of lubed beads into his anus, then slowly pull them out with each orgasmic contraction.

Note: Cotton cord anal beads are for one-time use only, since they can store bacteria, even after washing. Try nylon or silicone cords instead.

Sadie Sez:

Bead smooth. Before using plastic beads, always examine them thoroughly for any sharp edges that may need filing and smoothing.

Vibrating Anal-Ts

These innovative toys are designed to seek out your guy's prostate—and bring him to orgasm—because they're curved just right to land an exciting vibration just where he wants it.

Sadie Sez:

A sexy trick. Place a clean Anal-T inside your own backdoor during intercourse and he'll feel the vibrating tip inside on his penis with each stroke!

Strap-On Harnesses

He may be surprised—and you may be delighted—that sales of harnesses are booming among heterosexual couples all over America!

Has this crossed your mind? Strap-ons are designed to hold a dildo upright and rigid against your pubic bone. This enables you to penetrate your lover from behind, which can give him incredible prostate orgasms, and offer you the feeling of sexual authority—which can be very fulfilling and rewarding. ❤

 Sadie Sez:

Et tu? Every anal technique above, with the exception of prostate pleasure, will work for you, too. Interested? You know who to ask!

10

Ready...
Willing...
Unable...

Ahhh. Soft music. Soft candlelight. Soft breeze. Then, at the very height of passion...soft penis.

If a guy's little head can tell his big head what to do, watch how frazzled your guy becomes when he learns it doesn't work the other way around.

The truth is, penis mishaps, misfires and miscues affect every guy at one time or another. But the moment it happens to your guy, it can be an earth-shattering event.

Not-So-Easy To Be Hard

Since it's impossible for women to know how it feels to get an erection, it's even tougher to relate to losing one. It's something like trying to play a game of pool with a piece of rope.

Impotence—the inability to get or keep a good solid erection—can be caused by the body, the mind, or both. It can be rooted in depression, guilt, stress, anger or chronic illness. It can also be a result of street drugs or prescription drugs, alcohol, tobacco, advancing age—or even sitting too long on a bicycle seat.

Impotence is more common than you think. This means that at some point in your life, this deflator of sexual self-confidence will strike the guy you're with. The good news? In almost all guys, erections can be restored. So don't panic.

What Do *You* Do When He Goes Soft?

No matter what excuse he's muttering, fears and anxieties are undoubtedly racing through his mind, making it even harder for him to get, um, hard. Your best bet is to take a break to distract him and reestablish your connection. Tell him it's okay. Kiss. Cuddle. Keep the mood light. Relieve any guilt. Relax. And don't put any pressure on him to get hard again.

Ready...Willing...Unable...

Then try this:

- ♥ Play lovingly with his penis and balls, with no expectations. Touch lightly. Squeeze and release. Stroke with lube. Kiss him deeply.

- ♥ Admire him and his penis, and whisper adoring words. Tell him how good he makes you feel—without pressure or expectation his erection will return.

- ♥ Take his soft penis in your mouth. Even if this doesn't bring back a full erection, it will still feel warm and very nice.

- ♥ Move on to something playful...like light spanking!

If he doesn't get hard that day, try again another day. Never show disappointment, frustration or anger. He's a man—not a machine—with no control over his penis right now. Take the time to show him that he's much more to you than just a warm body part.

If the quality of his erections becomes an ongoing issue, try talking about it—openly and honestly—and be supportive of each other, especially if you don't know what's causing it. Then suggest he find out more by talking to a doctor, urologist or therapist.

Sadie Sez:

Call in the understudy. As a great relief for both of you, pull out your dildo or vibrator, and let him take care of you till his erection comes back. He should be happy to finish you off!

Pop A Pill—Get An Erection

For the first time in history, a guy can actually pop a pill and temporarily overcome impotence—without herbs, implants, pumps or voodoo.

Today's erectile dysfunction pills send blood to the penis, dilating the blood vessels when there is sexual stimulation. The blood is then sealed inside the penis, and *voila!*, a welcome erection.

If your guy decides to try one of them, keep in mind it's not an aphrodisiac, not a cure-all and there may be side effects. Read the literature carefully.

Sadie Sez:

Vacuum it up. Try a penis pump as a safe, fun alternative to pill popping (but never do them at the same time!)

Before trying this quick fix, your guy would be wise to find out if his situation is really a symptom of an underlying medical or psychological issue that these pills will only mask. Rule out any hidden conditions by talking to the appropriate doctor or therapist first.

Caution: NEVER mix erectile dysfunction pills with any other drugs without a doctor's approval.

Mr. Hair-Trigger

Since the sex techniques in this book are about penis pleasing and not intercourse, you'll never be left unsatisfied if he comes too quickly. Still, I'll bet you'd like him to enjoy more of your handiwork before the fireworks.

If it's all over too quickly, the solution may be helping him get more familiar with his point-of-no-return. This way, you can both learn to back off it slightly before it's too late, especially if he's young and still mastering his body. Try these techniques to put more time in his meter:

Green Light. Red Light. Stroke him until he tells you he's about to come—then stop—and wait till the feeling subsides. Now start again, stopping when he says he's getting close. Repeat several times. This will help him become more aware of his point-of-no-return, and know when to pause before it's too late.

The Headlock. When he's close to coming, place your thumb on his V-spot, and wrap your fingers around the other side of his shaft. Now squeeze gently and hold for a few seconds. This will help him suppress his orgasm. If he should come anyway, be sure to release your headlock and stroke him the way he likes—then try again next time.

Mind Game. Suggest that when he's about to come, to think about something stupendously non-sexual such as programming a VCR, finding a bug in a burrito, or the ever-popular baseball!

Taint Lock. When he feels like he's close to coming, place three fingers into the center of his taint and press firmly. It may take you a little practice to find the right spot, but you're trying to crimp the tube that carries the fluid from his prostate. Keep trying and don't give up!

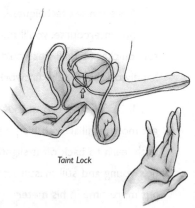

Taint Lock

To give you and your guy more stroke-to-orgasm time:

♥ **Relax.** As he approaches orgasm, ask him to slow down his rate of breathing with long inhales and exhales, and relax his tensing muscles. This can help him delay orgasm.

♥ **Master the PC muscle.** Strengthening his PC muscle can give him greater control, too. See page 23 for easy exercises he can do while watching TV.

♥ **Avoid alcohol and drugs.** They dull the self-awareness he needs to delay his hair-trigger.

♥ **Wrap up.** A condom (or two!) can slow orgasm. So can a penis sleeve.

♥ **Be comfortably numb.** Try applying a topical numbing cream designed to desensitize the head of the penis.

The Forever Man

Your wrist is breaking. Your jaw is aching. Your neck is shaking. And still no quake-ing. Why doesn't he come already?

Even if you've tried every rhythm, stroke and caress in the book, some guys just take a long long time. And some may never come at all. Maybe he needs intercourse. Maybe he can't come in a condom. Maybe he's more comfortable with his own hand. Or maybe he just needs time to build trust in you.

You shouldn't take this personally—you are arousing him. He's just unable to cross the finish line. Try asking him if there's anything else he'd like you to try. Perhaps he'd like to show you his favorite stroke himself. Maybe he's over-stimulated and needs a short break to reset. It could be a prescription medication causing the marathon. Or maybe he simply needs to focus his mind on you, and not life's stresses.

Be patient, talk about it, and work together to find your solution. ♥

 Sadie Sez:

Is he a frequent pickle pumper? If he masturbates at the drop of a hat, it could be his over-yanking thats desensitizing his penis to your mouth or vagina. Suggest he keep his hands off himself for a week or two, and see if his sensitive sensations return.

Appendix

Safer, Cleaner, Healthier Sex

With sex comes risk. No human being on earth is immune to today's menu of sexually transmitted diseases (STDs)—including you. You *must* protect yourself.

To practice safe sex means to keep the bodily fluids that can transmit STDs totally separate (blood, semen and vaginal juices). Being prepared shows that you are considerate and that you care about yourself.

Your safest path is to stay totally monogamous—and to get tested to be sure both you and your guy are free of any hidden STDs. But you'll still need to practice birth control to avoid unwanted pregnancies.

The good news is that many of the erotic techniques in this book are designed to keep sex about as safe as sex can get. You're pretty safe kissing, licking, nibbling, sucking and massaging your guy everywhere but his private parts. You're pretty safe giving him the wildest skin-on-skin handjobs you can dream up. And when he rolls on a latex condom, you're pretty safe giving him the world's most orgasmic blowjobs.

Practice Safe Condom Use

♥ **Roll a latex condom on him.** For all vaginal, anal—and yes, oral activities—insist he wear a condom.

♥ **Use a condom every time.** They're not only inexpensive, they're effective. Be sure he's wearing it correctly, too (see page 140).

♥ **Store your condoms wisely.** Keep a fresh supply on hand. Don't leave them in the heat or in a wallet. Never re-use them. And toss 'em after their expiration date. If you open one that looks or feels bad, don't use it.

♥ **Stay sober.** Drinking and recreational drugs weaken your assertiveness, lessen your ability to communicate, and make it tougher to focus on putting on a condom correctly. Know when to say 'when.'

Condom *What Ifs...*

What if either of you is allergic to latex condoms? It may be the latex, or the nonoxynol-9 spermicide already on the condom. Try a condom without this spermicide, or a polyurethane condom instead. But be aware: polyurethane is less elastic, so it breaks more often. Do not use condoms made of lambskin, since they will not block the transmission of STDs (but they do block sperm and work to prevent pregnancy).

What if he's uncomfortable in condoms? Try a variety—latex condoms are available in different shapes, sizes and thicknesses, from extra large to snugger fit to wider at the tip. Test-drive a few and find a new favorite!

What if he's uncircumcised? Gently pull back his fore-skin, and then unroll the condom to the base of his penis.

What if you want to share a sex toy? Germs can cling to porous toy surfaces, such as latex—so don't share! But if you do, put new condoms on your toys before each use.

What if you give a handjob without a condom? You're safe, as long as you don't have any fresh cuts, open sores or cracks from chapping on your hands.

What if I go down without him wearing a condom? You can catch a STD—even from his pre-come. Be sure he tests clean before taking this risk.

How To Roll-Out A Condom

Put it on him before there is any contact with your mouth, vagina or butt.

♥ Hold it by the tip to squeeze out the air.

♥ No reservoir tip? Leave about 1/2 inch of space at the tip for his come.

♥ Unroll it over his erect penis, all the way to the base.

♥ After he comes, and before he gets soft, hold the rim of the condom at the base to keep it from slipping off till he is away from you. Then gently remove the condom and flush it, or wrap it in a napkin and toss it in the garbage.

♥ Use a new condom to have sex again.

 Sadie Sez:

When lips meet latex. Pick up a plain, non-lubed condom. Before unrolling it, add a couple of drops of water-based lube inside the tip to create pleasurable friction for him. Then drizzle your favorite flavored lube on the outside for the best taste for you. Or try a flavored condom.

Enjoying Safer Anal Play

♥ **Latex.** For the safest finger play, slip into a pair of latex gloves—or try finger cots—latex finger sleeves. They protect against the spread of germs and can create slipperier, sexier sensations. Always use lube.

♥ **Dental dams.** Create a protective layer between you and your guy's erogenous zone for the safest tongue play. Use plastic wrap from your kitchen, or dental dams—which are rectangular pieces of latex you can buy at fine sex boutiques and online. Hold dental dams flat against the area you'd like to lick and caress and you're ready to go.

♥ **See Chapter 9** for more safety tips on backdoor play.

Be Clean. Be Safe. Be Happy.

Be sure to include these easy sexplay tips to keep you healthy:

♥ **Wash up.** Don't introduce germs from the outside world onto and into your most sensitive private parts. Before anyone touches anything, wash hands with soap and warm water. If he's uncircumcised, encourage him to wash under his foreskin—every day.

♥ **Clean your toys.** Before and after each use, wash your toys with water and antibacterial soap or an adult

toy cleanser. This will help prevent bacterial and yeast infections. You can sterilize silicone and glass dildos in boiling water for five minutes, or wash them on the top rack in your dishwasher. Dry your washed toys completely before storing them, or for the safest results, let them air-dry.

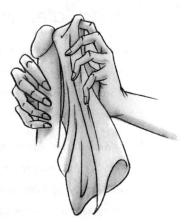

♥ **Examine your toys.** Check your toys carefully for sharp edges that can scrape, or splits that can hide bacteria. If you improvise your toys, double check that they're sturdy and won't break off inside either of you.

♥ **Clean your room.** Toss all towels you use for after-sex wash-up right into the laundry, or simply use tissues. Wash all bedsheets after you've messed them up, too. ♥

A AfterPlay

Congratulations! You're on the verge of graduating from Penis School. Just one more little detail before you can receive your Penis PhD...

Ravish your guy's penis.

Select an evening this week to spring your sexy surprise. Rivet his attention back on you. Revel in his rising passion. Rejoice till the very last drop.

After all, you deserve *all* the romance, affection and pleasure you'll get in return!

X's and O's,

Dr. Sadie Allison

Dr. Sadie

P.S. Let me hear from you! Share your tickled pickle tales with me. And if I use your story or technique in my next book, I'll send you an autographed copy, along with a very special toy!

Write to me at *ticklekitty.com* or
Tickle Kitty, 3701 Sacramento Street #107, San Francisco, CA 94118 USA

143

Special Thanks

To all my friends and peers who helped—you're the BEST:

Demetra Stevens—my straight-up bad-ass slickster, I knew I could count on you. **Mark Supachana**—we're gonna hit that million book mark yet! **Bo Pezulllo**—my loyal supporter, I adore you, xoxo BoBo. **Shelly Campbell & Michael Robles**—my horny friends who contributed a "load." **Jady Smith**—a beauty-ful star with shining input—thanks for a great job on my hair and makeup for the cover! **Darlene Vidmar**—a true home party expert. **Lisa Mazurek**—great tips and tricks inside! **Elizabeth Turecki**—killer stuff, girl! **Dr. Bruce Bakkar**—I'm spreading your message! **Vajra Haha**—tickled to have your Tantric touch! **Dave Guingona**—no cold hands, BABY! **Rick Sicurella**—always there for me, you're the best. **Catherine Duperret, Adria Avilla** and **Anthony Brown**—my faithful posse…it's vacation time! **Adam Carolla**—your penis quote ROCKS! **Sue Johanson**—you truly inspire me, thanks for the great quote and your continued belief in me. **Kristin Lippel & "J"**—love you always. **Randy Gulliver**—thanks for all you do. **The "Bob & Tom" Family**—my sincerest thanks for believing in me and helping me grow.

To my family—without you, I wouldn't be where I am today:

Jason, Justin, Joshua & Jazmin—*you're the BEST*. Thanks for your unconditional love! **Mom**—thanks for everything you do for me. I love you.

And my deepest thanks to the Tickle Kitty All-Stars:

Richard G. Martinez—You come through like a champ every time. You're an absolute genius with your creative direction and dazzling designs. No one could ever top your work.
Rich Lippman—your editorial work and research ability were outstanding, especially since the only penis you've ever touched is your own!
Steve Lee—you're the BEST illustrator! From female masturbation techniques to sex toys to dicks 'n licks…you always come through with amazing speed and outstanding representations.

Thank you all. ♥

About
^{The}Author

Dr. Sadie Allison's books, *Tickle Your Fancy, Toygasms!* and *Tickle His Pickle* instantly zoomed up the charts and became national bestsellers. Each received the prestigious Independent Publishers Best Sexuality Book Award. Dr. Sadie also formulated a high-end line of FDA-approved pleasure lubricants called *Slippery Kitty.*

Dr. Sadie educates millions on E! TV, *Talk Sex with Sue Johanson,* Discovery Health's *Berman & Berman*, Showtime, Dr. Drew's *Loveline,* Playboy TV, Howard Stern and more. She's a regularly quoted sex authority in *Cosmopolitan, Redbook, Glamour, Men's Health UK,* and is a sought-after speaker.

Dr. Sadie Allison is a graduate of San Diego State University with a B.A. in French and Marketing, and completed her Doctorate in Human Sexuality from the Institute for Advanced Study of Human Sexuality. She's a certified sexologist, member of the American Association of Sex Educators, Counselors & Therapists (AASECT) and is founder and Kitty-In-Chief of Tickle Kitty, Inc. She was born, raised, and still lives in the "city by the bay," and spends her days writing, jogging across the Golden Gate Bridge and hosting dinner parties with friends.♥

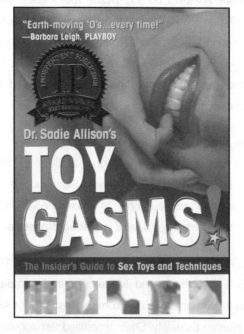

Pleasure at *your* fingertips

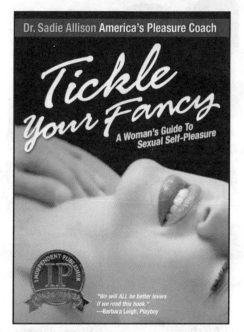

Tickle Your Fancy

The Number One guide to
female sexual self-pleasure.
by Dr. Sadie Allison

The lube requested by most penises!

Au Naturel™   *Strawberry Lust*™

Water-based. Condom-safe. Stain-free.

Let's click together

Dear Curious Guy,

You've got the coolest woman in the world. She's reading an erotic book about pleasing you and your penis—and now she's aiming to give you the strongest, wildest, most explosive orgasms of your life.

So just lie back and enjoy it, right?

Wrong!!! Take this erotic opportunity to rev up her passion, too. Try new moves. Touch. Tease. Talk. Laugh. Explore. Reciprocate. Tell her how fine her touch feels. Learn what she likes. Then do it. And do it some more.

Remember, she's newly inspired to go wild on you. Return her passion, or risk being left in the dust.

Love,

Dr. Sadie Allison

P.S. As long as you've got your nose in her book, here's everything she's too polite to tell you she doesn't like while she's pleasuring you:

(Ladies: check as many as apply.)

☐ Ear grabbing
☐ Deep thrusting
☐ Head guiding
☐ Hair pulling
☐ Finger clenching
☐ Gas passing

☐ Body odor
☐ Foreskin odor
☐ Locker room balls
☐ TV watching
☐ Falling asleep
☐ Mile-long pubic hairs

☐ Ass spanking
☐ Verbal ordering
☐ Excessive gyrating
☐ Being mouse-quiet
☐ _____
☐ _____